From Black to Biracial

FROM BLACK TO BIRACIAL

Transforming Racial Identity Among Americans

Kathleen Odell Korgen

PRAEGER

Westport, Connecticut
London

Library of Congress Cataloging-in-Publication Data

Korgen, Kathleen Odell, 1967–
    From black to biracial : transforming racial identity among
Americans / Kathleen Odell Korgen.
      p. cm.
    Includes bibliographical references and index.
    ISBN 0–275–95906–6 (alk. paper)—ISBN 0–275–96744–1 (pbk.)
    1. Racially mixed people—United States.   2. Ethnicity—United
States.   3. Racism—United States.   4. Interracial marriage—United
States.   5. Children of interracial marriage—United States—Race
identity.   6. United States—Race relations.   7. United States—
Ethnic relations.   I. Title.
E184.A1K733   1998
305.8′00973—dc21   97–34758

British Library Cataloguing in Publication Data is available.

Library of Congress Catalog Card Number: 97–34758
ISBN: 0–275–96744–1 (pbk.)

First published in 1998

Praeger Publishers, 88 Post Road West, Westport, CT 06881
An imprint of Greenwood Publishing Group, Inc.
www.praeger.com

Printed in the United States of America

The paper used in this book complies with the
Permanent Paper Standard issued by the National
Information Standards Organization (Z39.48–1984).

10 9 8 7 6 5 4 3 2 1

For Conor

Contents

Acknowledgments

I owe many thanks to the persons who worked "backstage" during the creation of this book. My husband Jeff motivated me constantly. He played a multifaceted role—husband, best friend, occasional editor, drill sergeant, and consistent supporter. He deserves to celebrate the completion of this book almost as much as I do.

Sy Leventman, David Karp, Jeane Guillemin, Karen Miller, and Mike Malec offered insightful commentary and enthusiasm. Lyn Rhenisch, Uli Boehmer, Patty Bergin, and James Vela-McConnell read, and reread, my work. James, in particular, devoted countless hours editing and helping me revise various drafts. I cannot imagine writing this book without him.

Valerie Odell and Patty Bergin provided invaluable assistance in finding interviewees. Valerie and my brother John provided the inspiration for this work—my wonderful nephew Conor. My parents showed me the merits and rewards of hard work. Judy and Ben Korgen, along with sending me pertinent news articles, gave me consistent and enthusiastic support. Alex del Carmen has proved to me the possibility of being both a great teacher and a true scholar. His success in both arenas continues to enliven me. My brother Michael has prayed hard for my success (as well as my salvation). Finally, my grandparents, John and Margaret McIntyre, provide stellar examples of lives worth leading. Their interest and pride in my work ensured the successful completion of *From Black to Biracial*.

From Black to Biracial

Introduction: The Transformation of Racial Identity

You can't avoid it. If you pick up a newspaper, or magazine, or turn on the television, it's there. Statistics, questions, and convictions emanate from every media outlet. How do you define race in a country in which racial mixing is increasingly common? Who is black? Who is Hispanic? Are Asian Americans becoming white? For that matter, what *is* white? These are just a sampling of the current racial identity questions now debated in the United States.

It is common knowledge that the United States is becoming increasingly diverse. According to demographer Leon Bouvier, "the United States is inexorably on its way to becoming a society with no one predominant group." By the middle of the twenty-first century, more than half of all Americans will be of non-European descent [1992:148].

These changing racial demographics affect the United States in a variety of ways. One significant aspect of this diversity is the rather sharp climb in the number of multiracial Americans. Race mixing, the subject of white supremacists' nightmares, is now an increasingly common occurrence in the United States. While, in 1970, 0.7 percent of all marriages in the continental United States were interracial, today 2 percent of all Americans marry outside their race [Marger, 1994]. "The number of . . . 'mixed-race' births have grown 26 times faster than all U.S. births" [Mills, 12/94–1/95:2]. These numbers make it clear that interracial couples and the children they produce must be given some serious attention by those who wish to understand our present and future society.

The extent of interracial marriages varies among racial groups. For instance, estimates of American Indian outmarriage[1] rates range from 40 to 78 percent. More than half of all Japanese Americans and more than 30 percent of Chinese Americans unite in marriage with someone from a different race (usually a white person). Thirty-five percent of Hispanics marry a non-Hispanic [Marger, 1994].

In our white-dominated society, it is the mixing of white and nonwhite blood that makes (and has made) many Americans feel uncomfortable. "Persons of color mixing with other persons of color—such as American Indians and blacks, Filipinos and Native Americans, Latinos and blacks—has been given little attention" by the white population [Root, 1992:6]. Anti-miscegenation laws were never aimed at these couplings. Intermarriage among persons of color does not challenge the existing hierarchy of races in which "pure" white is the pinnacle.

While non-African American minorities in the United States have faced discrimination ranging from genocide to everyday slights, the only group that was effectively and systematically enslaved in this country are African Americans. Restrictions on interracial fraternization necessary for the survival of race-based slavery followed by legal racial segregation may explain why African Americans would have the smallest outmarriage rate. Blacks (former slaves) and whites (former slave masters and otherwise racial oppressors) would be especially reluctant to intermarry with each other. Current interracial marriage figures support these suppositions. Just 3 percent of African Americans marry a nonblack person [Marger, 1994]. Only one in two hundred married couples consist of a black and a white person [Sándor, 6/94:38,39]. These figures indicate that taboos concerning interracial marriage between white and black Americans still persist.

In spite of all this, however, the interracial marriage rate between black and white Americans is increasing rapidly. In the last twenty-five years, the number of black/white interracial marriages has quadrupled. While in 1970 there were only 65,000 such couples, there were 246,000 in 1992 [Boston Globe, 1/18/95:28]. The growing numbers of the most tabooed romantic relationship—black and white—indicate the increasing instability of our present racial structure.

Throughout U.S. history, the children of black/white interracial couples have faced general degradation. Mixed-race persons have traditionally been portrayed in a negative light. In the first half of this century, reputable social scientists informed the public that such persons are "ungovernable" [Barzun, 1965:227]. American sociologist Edward Reuter determined that "the mixed blood is [always] an unadjusted person" [1918/1969:216]. The media have also flooded society with disturbing images of individuals with a mixed-race heritage. "Writers and filmmakers from Thomas Nelson Page to D.W. Griffith to William Faulkner have presented mixed people as tormented souls (Spickard, 1989:329–339)" [Spickard, 1992:20].

These images have promoted a very damaging picture of multiracial Americans. In Cynthia Nakashima's words:

Monoracial Americans have crafted a mythological multiracial monster who is genetically, mentally, culturally, socially, and politically distorted. The old cliché, 'What about the children?' is still the primary question posed to, or in many cases the primary condemnation aimed at, interracial couples in this country. [Nakashima, 1992:174]

With the historically negative image of biracial children, this seems to be a much-needed inquiry. How closely this picture fits reality, however, has yet to be the focus of an in-depth sociological study.

This book fills the gap in sociological research through an examination of the racial identity of black/white biracial Americans. Since the Voting Rights Act of 1965 signaled the culmination of the Civil Rights Movement, a transformation has occurred in the racial self-definition of Americans with both an African American and a white parent.[2] While the majority of such persons born immediately prior to the Movement perceive themselves as black, most young adult offspring of black/white couples define themselves as biracial. The following chapters address three primary issues: (1) the racial self-definition of biracial individuals, (2) influences on racial self-conception, and (3) the individual, social, and structural implications of this racial self-identity. This examination reveals the transformation in racial self-definition among biracial Americans and present and potential repercussions of this alteration in racial identity.

WHY IS A WHITE WOMAN INTERESTED IN BIRACIAL AMERICANS?

The particular subject of biracial Americans came to me through several powerful outlets. My brother Michael has Afghan and Iranian heritage. Two of my Irish Catholic uncles have married nonwhite women.[3] Some people joke that our family pictures resemble snapshots of the United Nations. A good number of my favorite relatives are non-white or mixed-race. Significantly, I cannot ever remember thinking about their race as I grew up. They were simply my brother, aunts, and cousins—people I enjoy being around. Now, as an adult focused on race relations in the United States, I realize the relative uniqueness of my family. Today I know enough to appreciate the racial diversity of my relatives and the lessons on racial tolerance and appreciation they unconsciously taught me.

This family history surely influenced my ability to embark on my own interracial relationship without hesitation. It did not, however, make me immune to the reservations of others. As a young single woman I was greatly affected by reactions of some friends and their parents when I dated a black man. Questions of "but what about your children?" arose before any serious thought of marriage entered my (or his, I'm sure) mind. While none of my close friends expressed disapproval, many spoke of how their own parents would not accept their dating a black man. I was disturbed that such views still existed.

My brother's marriage to a black woman strengthened my distaste for disapprovers. I was struck by a sense of ridiculousness. The social construction of a problem was never so obvious to me. In 1992, well over a century since the death of slavery and decades after the abolishment of legal segregation, few personal relationships exist between members of the black and white races. Today, with no legal impediments to interracial relationships, many persons still cling to traditional disapproval of them. The question "But what about the children?" merely helps give new life to, and reason for, this disapproval.

The birth of my nephew brought my feelings on this matter to the forefront. Here, in the flesh, was the child for which so many persons professed concern.

While I could answer with off-the-cuff responses to their fears for a hypothetical child, I wanted to do more for my nephew. I determined to find out what the world holds for a biracial boy born in the United States in 1993. More than anything else, I hoped to find that America had changed and become a more welcome place than the parents of my friends believed.

Blessed with a unique combination of brains, good looks, and charming personality, my nephew is a remarkable little boy. Able to read and count by the age of two, he freely shares his abundant love and affection. He makes friends with all whom he encounters. Computer literate, he is apt to stop and talk with laptop users he happens upon, discussing the merits of their computer in relation to his own. The first grandchild on his father's side, he is the light of our family.

This book grew out of my desire to understand what life will be like for my nephew as a biracial American. In my research and writing, I was very aware of my own white racial background. While realizing my perspective differs from that of biracial or black persons, I maintain that it is equally valid. The world can never be viewed "objectively" by anyone. Each person's perspective is grounded in his or her unique experiences. We can obtain the most objective picture possible when we take into account the views of multiple persons. My perspective is that of a white female sociologist personally concerned about my subject matter and trained in the art of social science research. While this was problematic for one of my interviewees, the vast majority did not indicate any unease with my whiteness.[4]

Recently there has been a surge of writing based on data derived directly from biracial individuals themselves. Such widely read works as *Black, White, Other* [Funderburg, 1994] and the magazines *Interrace* and *Biracial Child* are heartening and strong resources on this subject. However, sources such as these focus predominantly on individual stories of biracial people. There is still a relative dearth of sociological research on this group of Americans. This study is the first sociological examination of the changing dialectic between society and the racial identity of biracial individuals.

THEORETICAL PERSPECTIVE

The theoretical perspective of symbolic interactionism[5] structures the analysis in this book. Symbolic interactionists maintain that "human beings are symbol-using animals who collectively give meaning to the objects, events, and situations that make up their lives" [Karp and Yoels, 1993:2]. These meanings change from one particular group of people to another depending upon the time and social situation. For instance, concepts as various as "old," "successful," "yummy," and "high-powered" vary from society to society.

Race is also a social construction; it differs throughout space and time. For instance, "black" is defined very differently in Brazil than in the United States. Likewise, the idea of who is black, not to mention what it means to be black, has gone through many transformations throughout the history of this nation. This understanding, garnered through symbolic interaction, resonates throughout the following pages.

Race has always played a large role in social interaction in the United States. Along with gender, it is usually one of the first aspects we notice about a person. "We utilize race to provide clues about who a person is. The fact is made painfully obvious when we encounter someone whom we cannot conveniently racially categorize—someone who is, for example, [obviously] racially 'mixed.' . . . Such an encounter becomes a source of discomfort and momentarily a crisis of racial meaning" [Omi and Winant, 1986:60]. This makes it difficult for many Americans to "place" some individuals of mixed-race backgrounds into one of their compartments of racial stereotypes. For many, this promotes a sense of unease. It is ironic that this discomfort occurs when the biracial person has physical characteristics applicable to both whites and blacks. There are, however, many mixed-race people who appear to be either "all" white or "all" black.

According to Cooley's idea of the "looking glass self," we are what we think people see [1902]. This proves a dilemma for individuals of mixed race in a society in which racial stereotypes are rampant and usually automatic. People who view a biracial person may be frustrated in their efforts to fit that person into one of the United States' recognized racial categories. Because race is so enmeshed in people's impressions of others, this could prove disconcerting to both the mixed-race individual and the general public. According to Omi and Winant, "without a racial identity, one is in danger of having no identity" [1986:60]. In the same vein, a biracial person who is perceived to be either black or white is in danger of having a false social identity—one in which only half of their racial heritage is acknowledged.

Underneath this all, however, is the simple fact that "if a person, by birth, belongs to and identifies with more than one racial and cultural group, the monoracially 'hegemonic' American culture is forced either to adjust the system to make room for the person or to adjust the person to fit into the system" [Nakashima, 1992:164]. It is usually far easier to make an individual adjust rather than to alter an entire system. With the population of biracial Americans ever increasing, however, the system itself is becoming less stable. The following chapters delve into the historical relationship between biracial Americans and the racial structure of the United States through an examination of the transformation of racial identity among biracial Americans.

OVERVIEW

Chapter 1 places the present transformation of racial identity into historical context. In doing so, it answers such questions as: How long have biracial Americans existed in the United States? Has the manner in which biracial individuals have been perceived and treated in the United States undergone any previous transformations during the history of this nation? This chapter examines the history of biracial Americans through the changing lenses of law, class, culture, and religion.

To understand the present transformation better, we must contrast the personal stories of biracial adults who were born before the Civil Rights Movement with those who have just recently entered adulthood. Chapter 2 presents case studies of three biracial persons born, respectively, before, during, and after the Civil Rights era. These case studies reveal the transformation through the perspective of biracial persons themselves.

As Anselm Strauss declares, "it is not change that needs to be explained but its specific directions" [1959:43]. Why has the racial identity of black/white Americans moved from "black" to "biracial"? Chapter 3 discusses the direction of this transformation in racial identity, drawing out the influences of history, culture, immediate social setting, and racial appearance.

Chapter 4 explores how the transformation influences the personal lives of young biracial Americans. Racial tension and division exist on most college campuses today. When blacks and whites are polarized, where does this leave the biracial student? Many monoracial college students view biracial persons' dating choices as indicative of their racial identity. In turn, biracial college students find whom they date to be a litmus test of their racial self-definition. Many face severe pressure from both white and black students to make the "correct" racial choice in dating partners. This chapter examines the dating experiences and ensuing racial dilemmas of biracial college students.

Chapter 5 turns to the basic question of whether or not biracial Americans are "marginal" people. Are they both "not quite black enough" around African Americans and "not quite white enough" around white Americans? Robert Park's definition of the "marginal man" is utilized in this determination of the extent to which biracial persons experience marginality.

Along with questions of marginality, biracial persons must deal with the fact that there is no official "biracial" racial classification. Many monoracial persons maintain that a biracial person cannot have a true racial identity. Today, however, many once stable identities are now in flux. Persons now choose identities that were once ascribed. Individuals and societies are now transforming gender and sexuality as well as race. A theory of identity must incorporate this new reality. Chapter 6 describes a new theory of identity based on the works of both symbolic interactionist and postmodern theorists. The transformation of racial identity among biracial Americans is a case study of this societywide phenomenon of increasing fluidity of identities.

An example of this fluidity is the current attempt to revise the U.S. Census. The manner in which the 2000 Census will define the population is currently a matter of fierce debate. Those with more than one racial background have been among the loudest of those engaged in this battle. The outcry of many biracial Americans against having to declare themselves as solely black, solely white, or "other" has grown too loud for census takers and politicians to ignore. On the other hand, existing affirmative action programs, federal aid, and our entire racial structure hinge upon the maintenance of the present Census definitions of race. Chapter 7 examines the public policy implications of the transformation.

While today mixed-race Americans challenge the very foundation of our racial structure, such persons have existed in this country for almost four centuries. In fact, the first biracial Americans were born before clear distinctions were made between blacks and whites. We now turn to this time before racial classifications existed. The setting is early colonial America, a period in which class distinctions were paramount. People were simply masters or servants regardless of their skin color.

NOTES

1. In this instance, "outmarriage" refers to marrying outside one's racial group.

2. In the United States, the determination of who is black and who is white is based on a social construction of race [Davis, 1991]. There is no biologically precise way to distinguish between the races. For the sake of simplicity, throughout this book "biracial" refers to those with both a black and a white parent. Parents are identified as "black" according to the interviewee's conception of what society perceived the race of the parent to be. The same type of definition is utilized in the identification of the "white" parents.

3. Interestingly both were Peace Corps volunteers and spent time in countries in which they, as white men, were members of the racial minority. This may have played a role in their ability to view members of other races as equals and suitable marriage partners.

4. I discuss my experience as a white interviewer in more detail in the Appendix.

5. For a thorough description of this theory see Blumer, 1969.

1
Biracial Americans: White, Black, Both, Neither

In 1630, a mixed crowd of Africans and white Virginia colonists assembled to see Hugh Davis, a white man, severely beaten with a whip. His crime was having sex with an African woman. The colonial leaders deemed this act a "dishonor of God and shame of Christians" [Williamson, 1980:7]. These leaders hoped that his whipping and subsequent public acknowledgment of his "fault" would discourage any further sexual intercourse between English colonists and Africans. While there is no clear record of whether this strategy worked with the beaten Hugh Davis, it is quite apparent that the overall effort was a failure. Miscegenation between blacks and whites, and the subsequent creation of biracial persons, has been a consistent and integral part of colonial and U.S. history.

The history of biracial Americans begins soon after the arrival of the first Africans in North America. In 1619, a Dutch man-of-war gave the English colonists of Virginia twenty Africans in exchange for food supplies. Shortly thereafter, the first black-white biracial individuals were born in what is now the United States. Africans worked side by side with indentured servants from England. Enduring similar hardships and demeaning labor, the white and black field hands became friends and, in some cases, lovers.

Over the years, the manner in which biracial individuals have been perceived and treated in the United States has undergone various transformations. Factors that have propelled these transformations include the American institutions of law, class, culture, and religion. This chapter examines the history of biracial Americans through the changing lenses of these institutions.

1619–1776: THE COLONIAL YEARS

For approximately forty years, African and white servants were treated with equal harshness under the law. Over time, however, white and black labor became distinguished from each another. White indentured labor dwindled, while African labor became transformed into slavery. The decision to establish African slavery inalterably affected the relations between blacks and whites in the United States. In turn, it played a direct role in how black-white biracial Americans have been perceived and treated.

The choice of using Africans as slave labor was based on both pragmatic and religious reasoning. According to Lerone Bennett [1987:44], "a worldwide demand for sugar and tobacco and the development of capitalist planting techniques based on the use of gang labor . . . tilted the structure in the direction of black slavery." The English were desperate for cheap and reliable labor. Using white servants had resulted in limited success. There was a scarcity of British subjects who were interested in or available to be coerced to travel across the wide ocean to work in the fields of North America. Moreover, it was against the religion of the English to enslave Christians, so the indentured servants ultimately had to be set free. The English had attempted to force the natives to work for them but it was too difficult to keep American Indians enslaved. European-bred diseases wiped out the majority of the native population. Those who survived knew the surroundings so well they could escape with relative ease. The captive and vulnerable Africans, neither native nor Christian, seemed to be the ideal solution to this labor shortage.

Some aspects of the Christian religion encouraged the acceptance of Africans as slaves. While Englishmen in the colonial era would not permit a fellow English Christian to be enslaved, they did "possess a concept of slavery" that could be used to rationalize African slavery. "This idea was formed by the clustering of several rough but not illogical equations. The slave was treated like a beast. Slavery was inseparable from the evil in men; it was God's punishment upon Ham's[1] prurient disobedience. Enslavement was captivity, the loser's lot in a contest of power. Slaves were infidels or heathens. On every count, Negroes qualified" [Jordan, 1968:56].

Once slavery was established, traditions that might stand in its way were quickly abolished. In 1667, Virginia passed a law that proclaimed a person could be both a Christian and a slave. This was done to discourage slaves from converting in order to be freed. In 1670, a law was passed that declared any non-Christian servant arriving in Virginia by ship subject to spend the rest of his/her life as a slave. At the time, Africans were the only non-Christians coming to America [Russell et al., 1992:10].

In order to rationalize and promote black slavery, the leaders of the colonies developed the idea that blacks were inferior and broke "the bonds of community between black and white servants, who constituted the majority of the population" [Bennett, 1987:45]. The first colonists did not have conceptions of "white" and "black" [Bennett, 1987:40]. Society was divided merely between servants and masters. African and European servants, in the first half of the seventeenth century, were treated as equals. In order for black slavery to work, however, ideas of race inferiority and superiority based on color had to be devised and promulgated. White workers had to be convinced that they had nothing in common with the black Africans. The religious climate of the colonies encouraged such distinctions between the races.

Religious leaders had attempted to separate the white Christians and the "heathen" Africans even before slavery was an issue. Sexual interaction between the races was especially frowned upon. The colonial leaders made many efforts to curb miscegenation. Records of colonial times brim with attempts to halt black-white procreation. In 1622, Virginia declared that "sex with Negroes was equivalent to bestiality" [Russell et al., 1992:13]. One of the oldest entries, written in 1630, focuses on the previously mentioned Virginian named Hugh Davis who was "to be soundly whipped, before an assembly of Negroes and others for abusing himself to the dishonor of God and shame of Christians, by defiling his body in lying with a Negro, which fault he is to acknowledge next Sabbath day" [Williamson, 1980:7].

The status of the offspring of interracial unions was a persistent problem for the leaders of the new colonies. Women constituted a small minority of the population in the colonies. Even among slaves, there was a much higher percentage of men than women. Therefore, the majority of the biracial children born had a white father and a black mother. English law had historically relegated all children to the status of their fathers. However, if this were to be the case in the colonies, it would prevent landowners from using many of the progeny of their slaves as labor. The Virginia Assembly addressed this concern by declaring in 1662 that biracial children of slave women were slaves [Williamson, 1980:7].

Biracial children with a white mother and a black father were another difficult concern of the leading colonists. If slavery were to be aptly defended, the races must be kept separate and distinct. Punishments were severe for any white women who delivered a child with a trace of African blood. In the late 1600s, fines and years of forced servitude were the fate of white women who gave birth to biracial children. Blacks and whites who chose to marry were banished from the colony of Virginia. By 1705, interracial couples who married were subject to prison terms of six months [Williamson, 1980:8, 11].

Between 1691 and 1725, Virginia, Massachusetts, North Carolina, South Carolina, Delaware, and Pennsylvania established anti-miscegenation laws [Bennett, 1987:301]. "Although these laws differed in detail, they generally extended the time of white servants who married black men or gave birth to mulatto children. Free white men and women who married blacks were fined, jailed or reduced to servitude; free blacks[2] who stepped across the color line were reduced to slavery or sold out of the colonies. Ministers and other persons who performed interracial marriages were required to pay fines of fifty pounds or so" [Bennett, 1987:303].

There is much evidence that interracial marriages persisted, however. A short time after Virginia established its anti-miscegenation law, an "Ann Wall was convicted of 'keeping company with a Negro under pretense of marriage.' The Elizabeth County Court sold Ann Wall for five years and bound out her two mulatto children for thirty-one years. And 'it is further ordered,' the court said, 'that if ye said Ann Wall after she is free from her master doe at any time presume to come into this county she shall be banished to ye Island of Barbadoes'" [Bennett, 1987:303]. Clearly, the colonial leaders employed harsh measures in their efforts to prevent interracial matrimony.

In many cases interracial unions took place outside the bonds of marriage. Some of these affairs led to the termination of the marriages of white men and women. Court records reveal that some white colonists demanded divorces based on their spouse's infidelity in the arms of a black person. A white woman's infidelity with a black man was often revealed through the birth of a dark-skinned child. One court entry noted that "a Westfield, Massachusetts man won a divorce in 1750 on a complaint that his wife Agnes had borne a child for a black man named Primus. Also, in 1751, the Massachusetts legislature dissolved the marriage of Lois Way, who had mothered a child by a slave named Boston" [Bennett, 1987:304]. Obviously, it was much easier for a white man to cover up any interracial affairs he might have.

In keeping with the goal to distinguish between whites and blacks, free biracial individuals were gradually stripped of their rights in the late 1600s and early 1700s. By 1723, the Virginia Assembly refused mixed-race persons the right to vote. The process of emancipation by private owners was made more arduous. No longer could slaves be freed simply at the immediate whim of their master. The rest of the colonies followed the lead of Virginia and enacted similar legislation [Williamson, 1980:10]. However, in spite of great efforts to prevent miscegenation, records indicate that there were approximately 60,000 biracial individuals in the former colonies by the end of the Revolutionary War [Reuter, 1918/1969:112].[3]

1776–1850: THE ANTEBELLUM YEARS

American independence brought about great upheaval in the area of rights and restrictions for biracial individuals. During this period, economic reality and ideological convictions resulted in the emancipation of large numbers of slaves, both black and mixed race. By the time of the American Revolution it was clear that slavery was not an economic necessity in the North. There was an abundant population of landless white persons who could fill the role of a servant class. Moreover, with the acceptance of revolutionary themes of "freedom and justice for all," slavery also began to appear startlingly hypocritical to increasing numbers of American citizens. The combination of these two factors, economic and moral, prompted many Northerners to free their slaves. By the first decade of the nineteenth century, Northern states legally prohibited slavery. New York, which was the last Northern state to pass legislation against slavery, eradicated the institution within its borders in 1804 [Franklin, 1980:93]. In the South, the clear economic profitability of slavery overwhelmed any moral hesitations about the institution. From the time of the Revolution, slavery became a particularly Southern manifestation.

With the freedom of so many black slaves, in some cases it became difficult to determine who was free and who was a slave. Moreover, as the manumitted (freed) population became increasingly black, many whites moved to increase the social, political, and economic distance between whites and free blacks. States codified definitions to designate clearly who was a Negro and who was not. Most states in the upper South drew definitions similar to Virginia's, which declared in 1785 that a Negro is "a person with a black parent or grandparent" [Williamson, 1980:13].

The history of biracial individuals differs in the upper and the lower South. During the Antebellum period, the upper South consisted of Virginia, Kentucky, Missouri, Maryland, Delaware, North Carolina, Tennessee, and the District of Columbia. The lower South was comprised of Florida, Texas, South Carolina, Georgia, Mississippi, Alabama, and Louisiana. Biracial people existed in the upper South since shortly after the first Africans arrived in 1619. Free mixed people in the upper South normally lived in rural areas [Spickard, 1989:247,248]. They were primarily the offspring of the lowest status members of society. Due in part to their association with their lower-class colonial forebears, they were treated by most members of white society as if they were black and tended to be marginal both economically and legally. "Throughout the rest of the United States, mulattoes had the same disadvantages as in the Upper South because they were grouped with blacks as a whole. Rarely anywhere did mulattoes have suffrage" [Zack, 1993:81].

Mixed-race persons did not exist in great numbers in the lower South until the eighteenth and nineteenth centuries. Even then they were not as numerous as those in the upper South. In 1850, the upper South had approximately two hundred thousand mixed race persons, while only about ninety thousand persons of mixed racial heritage lived in the lower South [Spickard, 1989:247]. The majority of those in the lower South were the offspring of prosperous white fathers and slave women. Many were acknowledged by their fathers. Most, however, were not manumitted in great numbers (about one in ten in 1850). The majority of those who were free "lived in the cities of New Orleans, Charleston, Mobile, and Savannah, where they formed a middle tier between White and Black, free and slave" [Spickard, 1989:248].

In the major cities of the lower South, there was a clear distinction between blacks and those of both African and European descent. In the lower South many mixed-race persons were, in fact, in a different caste than blacks. "The topmost few, the lightest and the brightest, quite literally the crème de la crème, lived very well—nearly on par with their white neighbors, to whom they were tied by bonds of kinship and culture" [Williamson, 1980:14,15]. This alliance of mixed-race persons with whites provided a buffer between the multitude of slaves and the outnumbered plantation owners. In cases of racial unrest the white population could count on the loyalty of the mixed-race population.

In South Carolina, by the time of the Revolutionary War, there were three blacks for every one white [Williamson, 1980:16]. Always fearful of slave uprisings, the white plantation owners encouraged the creation of a unique class of mixed-race people that might shield them from the black masses. A scarcity of white women also influenced the creation of a sizable mixed-race population. Many of those from a mixed racial background took advantage of their status in the lower South to achieve financial gain and some degree of social prominence. In fact, some mixed race families ran plantations and were slave owners themselves [Zack, 1993:81].

In Southern cities with large numbers of mixed-race persons, such as Charleston, Mobile, and New Orleans, some free females of predominantly white descent were able to use their beauty and their reputation as "exotic" to become informal "wives" to wealthy, white Southern gentlemen. For instance, "in the antebellum period, young New Orleans bachelors could shop for placées, stunningly attractive black women, well educated and trained in the art of casual domesticity, at the Quadroon Balls, held at the Salle d'Orleans" [Bennett, 1987:312]. These balls were "attended only by white men and light-skinned free women of color" [Spickard, 1989:243]. Many of these women, themselves offspring of white men and light-skinned black women, were sent to Paris and well educated in the feminine refinements of the day such as how to give a party, speak French, and play the piano. These young women were chaste and without visible African heritage. While law forbade them to marry white males, a tradition grew in which they were trained to become refined women and lovers of these same men. Their mothers would bargain with an interested white suitor. If he agreed to support the young woman in a comfortable fashion, a deal would be made in which the young mixed-raced female became the "kept" woman of the white man. In many instances, this relationship remained constant even after the man married in "respectable" society [Reuter, 1930/1970:42–44].

In keeping with the idea of establishing a "buffer" class, some authorities in South Carolina were reluctant to designate people of mixed race as black. In 1835, William Harper, a South Carolina judge, refused to determine whether a person of mixed race should be defined as black. He stated that "the condition of the individual is not to be determined solely by distinct and visible mixture of negro blood, but by reputation, by his reception into society, and his having commonly exercised the privileges of a white man." In other words if he acts like a "white" man, he should be treated as if he is a "white" man [Williamson, 1980:18,19] or, at least as was the case in many instances, as a "step up" from a black man.

1850–1910: FROM ABANDONMENT BY WHITES TO EMBRACING BLACKNESS

By the middle of the nineteenth century, however, the outlook for those of both black and white descent was decidedly grim. Mixed-race slavery was expanding on the frontiers, and manumission of any slaves was becoming increasingly rare. With the halting of the importation of slaves by the Slave Act of 1807 and the spread of slavery due to the Louisiana Purchase of 1803, the domestic slave trade had begun to blossom. Existing slaves became the primary stock of slave traders. As a result, by the mid-1800s, slaves became increasingly mixed. Meanwhile, as slavery came under continued assault, white Southerners closed ranks. Mixed-race free men and women were left out in the cold. They began to be looked upon with increasing suspicion.

The development of scientific racism in the nineteenth century led to the further denigration of blacks and extreme white opposition to black/white interracial relationships [Kinney, 1985:21]. The pervasive eighteenth- and nineteenth-century scientific notion that natural order is based on inequality promoted arguments that justified slavery. Many scientific and medical experts of the day wrote scholarly pieces on the benefits of slavery for those of African descent.

One leading pro-slavery scholar was Samuel Cartwright. As the chair of a committee assembled by the Medical Association of Louisiana "to report on the 'diseases and physical peculiarities of the Negro race,' [he] presented the committee's findings in a southern medical journal." Among other deficiencies in blacks, Cartwright surmised that the "insufficient supply of red blood, when conjoined with the smaller brain and excess nervous matter, constituted the 'true cause . . . of that debasement of mind' in blacks." Slavery, though, provided some hope for the future health of blacks. When forced to work, their blood was "vitaliz[ed] . . . more perfectly." According to Cartwright, "slavery . . . improved blacks 'in body, mind and morals'" [Tucker, 1994:14].

It was the increasingly supported notion of the genetic differences between whites and blacks which made slavery ethically, as well as economically, defensible. Scientific racism also helped to increase the distinction in the minds of "pure" white people between themselves and those of any African descent. No longer did many whites view mixed-race people as "almost white." Instead, "mixed blood was associated with physical debility, mental inferiority, and moral degeneracy" [Zack, 1993:122].

It was made increasingly clear to those of mixed-race descent that white persons were not their sincere allies. In times of racial tension, in the eyes of whites, all mixed-race persons were black. Williamson, in *New People* [1980:66], describes the change in race relations in an area in the lower South that traditionally promoted a three-tier racial hierarchy. He writes that in Louisiana "free mulattoes and whites lived easily together into the 1850s; then radical agitation began against the 'free people of color.' . . . Whites [were] activated by a new fear of abolitionism and insurrection. The great fear of slaveholders grew into unrequited hatred as the decade preceding the Civil War progressed." As the Civil War approached, white fear of the fall of slavery prompted a fierce Southern defense of the "peculiar institution." The inferiority of blacks was vigorously promoted and used to defend African slavery. As abolitionist voices became louder, slaveholders became paranoid of potential threats to their way of life. Those who advocated freedom for blacks or, even more horrifying, the miscegenation of the races became suspect. Mixed-race persons, living testimony to the fact that interracial sex was taking place, began to be looked upon with increasing disdain and disgust. Efforts were made to distinguish more clearly between whites and those who had African ancestors.

As rules became more stringent and were more often enforced against those of both black and white descent, people of mixed race no longer turned their sympathies towards the whites around them. Instead, they moved slowly towards an uncomfortable alliance with blacks. While most regarded themselves as superior to blacks, they simply had nowhere else to turn when their former white allies spurned them.

Emancipation brought with it both great hopes and great trepidation for those of mixed-race descent. Those who were newly freed rejoiced, while those who had already been free men and women feared the loss of their status. In order to distinguish themselves from the newly freed slaves, color became an even more important signifier among the previously freed mixed-race population. Societies were formed in which only those light enough to pass such obstacles as the "brown paper bag," the "blue vein," and the "comb"[4] tests were allowed entrance. The mixed-race people who comprised these groups did all they could to separate themselves from common black people. "Although they were not white, they could thank God that they were not black" [Frazier, 1965:117].

A disproportionately large number of the black political leaders who came to power during the period of Reconstruction were of both white and African racial descent. "Fully three-quarters of the top-level Negro leaders in Reconstruction were visibly mulatto, while the national proportion of Negroes who were visibly mulatto was about 15 percent." Many were the sons of former prominent plantation owners. According to Joel Williamson, "it was almost as if mixing of this special sort in late slavery had produced a new breed, preset to move into the vanguard of their people when freedom came" [1980:56]. As youth, many of these leaders were granted special favors and training because of their intimate connection with their masters. Fine educations and social skills were common among the mixed-raced leaders. No doubt these attributes encouraged both their ability to lead and also the notion among the black masses that they should lead the newly freed slaves.

Shortly after the Civil War, however, black persons of all hues had further reason to band together. Upon passage of the 13th, 14th, and 15th Amendments, poor whites and freed slaves became economic competitors. No longer legally bound to their former masters, former slaves were potentially free to learn various trades and earn a decent wage. Economically disadvantaged Southern whites dreaded the possibilities. The freedom of former slaves "removed the ability of white workers to derive satisfaction from defining themselves as 'not blacks' and called into question self-definitions that centered on being 'not Black'" [Roediger, 1991:170]. Former slaves could become more successful than they were! At the very least, they would most likely flood the market with their labor, resulting in declining wages and jobs for whites. Seeking to diminish the bright prospects for those of African descent and ensure black inferiority, the poor whites formed a powerful coalition with those whom they used to resent—the former plantation owners. Their rage and embitterment focused on those with any African heritage.

With the presidential compromise[5] election of Rutherford B. Hayes in 1876 and the political revival of the Southern landed class, the fate of the former slaves was sealed. White America had joined forces to keep black America in the Southern cotton fields. States passed laws that severely curtailed the freedom of those of African descent. With the free flow of European immigrants into the Northern factories and the dearth of immigrants interested in settling in the South, the business communities of both the North and the South needed the labor of former slaves in the agriculturally based South. Aside from requiring labor to rebuild its wartorn and destitute land, the South needed cotton to be planted and picked while the Northern textile factories needed a steady, affordable supply of raw material. In order to ensure that blacks would till the Southern fields, "a system of contract labor[6] [was devised] that reduced the black population of the South to a state of virtual peonage" [Steinberg, 1989:192]. The vast majority of black Americans were newly enslaved through the only life made available to them—sharecropping.

As Reconstruction ended and restrictions on all those with any African heritage became increasingly severe, the former distinction between blacks and mixed-race persons began to close. Gradually, those of mixed racial background came to understand that, no matter how brown instead of black they appeared, they would always be seen as black by the white population. The "one drop rule"[7] had begun to take effect. "In white eyes, all Negroes came to look alike" [Williamson, 1980:62].

1910–1960: THE JIM CROW YEARS

Conversely, in the black and mixed-race world, their descendants did begin to look similar, at least in terms of skin color. During the first three decades of the twentieth century, an explosion of black unity and pride occurred. Besieged by white racism, those of African descent banded together and began to explore and rejoice in their racial heritage.

Marcus Garvey's Universal Negro Improvement Association, formed in 1914 in Jamaica, gained enormous popularity during this era. A Jamaican by birth, Garvey emphasized racial pride among Negroes, forcefully declaring blackness a sign of beauty and nobility. Maintaining that there was no chance that white Americans would ever treat African Americans with equality and dignity, he advocated that all black Americans should return to Africa. Garvey's followers were predominantly unschooled and lower-class African Americans. While most were unwilling to relocate to Africa, Garvey's ideas of black pride did move them. He made them proud of themselves and their racial heritage amidst a nation that scorned them.[8]

Middle-class and intellectual African Americans also bonded with their fellow black Americans during this period. The Harlem Renaissance was led by this group of African Americans. During these three decades, the mixed-race population no longer focused their energies on distinguishing themselves from dark-skinned blacks. Instead, they began to form an alliance with these same blacks. The mixed-race elite began to lead and "raise up" the black race. They also began to intermarry with dark-skinned blacks whom they had previously scorned.

Mixed-race people led the Harlem Renaissance. Langston Hughes, Jean Toomer, Countee Cullen, James Weldon Johnson, Walter White, and W.E.B. Du Bois all had various degrees of white ancestry. Unlike the majority of their forebears, however, these mixed-race men focused on their blackness rather than their whiteness. Light-skinned blacks married dark-skinned blacks. Lightness was no longer seen as something necessarily good. The black race became brown during these decades. "It is estimated that by 1918 seventy-five percent of black Americans were actually of mixed racial background" [Williamson, 1980:111]. The vast majority of this percentage grew out of mixed-race/black intermarriage.

It is important to note, however, that color consciousness never completely left the black community. Indeed, it was a topic of many of the Renaissance writers (e.g., Countee Cullen and Nella Larsen). The very fact that most of the black leaders were (and still are) light-skinned leads one to question the success of the intra-black anti-racism movement. There was, however, a concerted effort made by many African American leaders of the day to curb the preoccupation with skin color and concentrate, instead, on empowering the black community as a whole. Prior and parallel to the Harlem Renaissance was the construction and perpetuation of the legal segregation of the black and white races. By 1910, the Jim Crow[9] system was firmly established. The law now enforced what social custom in the South had demanded. The separation between whites and blacks was clearly defined in all aspects of life.

The vast majority of society frowned upon any type of interracial fraternization. Both keepers of the law and of social etiquette strictly monitored any social interaction between the two races. At this point in history, anyone socializing with blacks was susceptible to the charge of being a "white nigger." People were convinced that if you "acted" black you were black [Williamson, 1980:98–108].

It was quite clear during this period that anyone with any African ancestry was black. Once they accepted this blackness, however, individuals of mixed-race descent were "well regarded by both blacks and whites—blacks made them their leaders, and whites accepted them as black leaders" [Zack, 1993:114]. Almost all of the "Talented Tenth,"[10] the most important members of the black community, were of mixed race descent. "In 1918, Edward Reuter published his findings that 3,820 of 4,267 Negroes who had 'made any marked success in life' were mulattoes" [Williamson, 1980:129]. Indeed, Reuter went on to say that "the chances of the mulatto child developing into a leader of the race are thirty-four times as great as are the chances of a black child" [Reuter, 1918/1969:314].[11] Both blacks and whites viewed mixed-race persons as the natural leaders of the black community.

By the first decades of this century, even those who kept official records were clear in their understanding of how the black and white races in the United States are to be distinguished. Since 1920, the Census has determined black people to be "all persons with any known black ancestry" [Davis, 1991:11].[12] "The nation's answer to the question 'Who is Black?' has long been that a black is any person with any known African black ancestry. . . . This American cultural definition of blacks is taken for granted as readily by judges, affirmative action officers, and black protesters as it is by Ku Klux Klansmen" [Davis, 1991:5].

Accepting the terms of the "one drop rule," the light-skinned leaders of the black community turned their energies to raising up the black race. One powerful example of a mixed-race leader who embraced the cause for black rights was Walter White, the famous executive secretary of the NAACP (National Association for the Advancement of Colored People) in the second third of this century. White, appearing in all respects to be a white man, was 5/32 black. "In Melville J. Herskovits' often-quoted words, 'Two human groups never meet but they mingle their blood.' And of course, this has always been the case in the United States. But due to the alchemy of American racism, no new race ever results. Black and white do not make gray here, but black" [Zack, 1993:171]. In Walter White's case, white and black, and white and white, and white and white . . . do not make white, but black.

With the emphasis on the one drop rule and clear social and legal distinctions made between blacks and whites, there was little social interaction between whites and black Americans in the first half of this century. Interracial relationships between white and African Americans were relatively unheard of during that time. It was not until the 1960s that interracial marriages began to occur in significant numbers. According to a Gallup poll, as late as 1958, 92 percent of Northern and Western whites and 99 percent of Southern whites were opposed to interracial marriages [Spickard, 1989:292,293]. Blacks also disapproved of mixed-race unions. They believed that it was predominantly the lowest of both classes who would engage in interracial relationships. Both blacks and whites looked upon the obvious offspring of such couplings, light-skinned blacks, as low class and "associated with sin and degradation" [Davis, 1991:57].

Blacks who dated or married whites often faced ostracism from the African American community. "Lena Horne's family stopped talking to her when she married white bandleader Lennie Hayton. And shortly after the Brown decision against segregated schooling, a Black college president expelled one of his Black students for dating one of the new Whites on campus" [Spickard, 1989:301].

In the early to mid-1900s, the children of interracial couples grew up in a generally hostile world. While the black half of the family generally lacked enthusiasm about the marriage, they tended to accept it and the ensuing offspring more than white relatives. Biracial children who were born before the sixties were, for the most part, not accepted by the white sides of their families. "Almost none of the more than three hundred Chicago mulattoes Robert Roberts interviewed in the 1930s, '40s, '50s had ever enjoyed a close relationship with his or her White grandparents, and most had no such relationship at all (this situation improved slightly in the 1960s)" [Spickard, 1989:330]. For many biracial children, the white side of their extended family either completely abandoned them or functioned merely as a painful reminder of racial division and disharmony within the family.

1960–1997: FROM THE CIVIL RIGHTS ERA TO THE PRESENT

At one point or another in U.S. history, thirty-eight states have passed anti-miscegenation laws [Sickels, 1972:1–10]. In some instances, couples were literally roused from their bed and arrested. In 1959, one such case involved a husband and wife from the state of Virginia. Richard Perry Loving, a white man, and Mildred Jeter, a woman of African and Native American descent, had obtained a legal marriage in neighboring Washington, D.C. Believing they had not broken the law since they had taken their marriage vows in Washington, the two were rudely surprised when they were awakened and arrested in the middle of the night for violating the state of Virginia's anti-miscegenation laws. Unbeknownst to them, the state law included a decree that disallowed Virginia couples to marry across racial lines out of state and then return to Virginia to reside.

The Virginia judge in the Loving case was a fierce defender and enactor of anti-miscegenation legislation. In addition to stating the fact that Virginia state law forbade whites and blacks from intermarrying, the judge reasoned that this decision reflected God's intentions. "Almighty God created the races white, black, yellow, malay, and red, and he placed them on separate continents. And but for the interference with his arrangement there would be no cause for such marriages. The fact that he separated the races shows that he did not intend for the races to mix" [quoted in Henriques, 1975:25]. The Lovings were given the choice of either leaving the state for twenty-five years or serving a prison sentence [Henriques, 1975:30]. This decision was merely one in a long list of cases in which anti-miscegenation legislation was upheld by state supreme court decisions.

However, despite still relatively high levels of social disapproval, increasing numbers of Americans have initiated interracial relationships. Several structural and cultural reasons contribute to this increase in cross-racial couplings. The first and foremost legal influence is the 1967 Supreme Court decision to overturn the *Loving v. Commonwealth of Virginia* verdict and invalidate laws that made interracial marriage a crime. Sixteen states still had anti-miscegenation legislation in 1967. An increase in interracial marriages followed the Loving verdict that repealed this legislation. A "biracial baby boom" began shortly thereafter. Close to fifty thousand children were born to black/white, interracial marriage partners in 1990 alone [Sándor, 6/94:38,39].[13] The legalization of interracial marriage granted people all across the United States the legal sanction to marry whomever they choose (assuming they were heterosexual). With this decision, interracial marriage could no longer be viewed as deviant behavior.

Deviant behavior itself was touted during the decade of the sixties. Protests from sit-ins to draft card burnings flourished during that era. Tradition was suspect.

Many of the youth of the day came to the conclusion that following the status quo had produced both oppression at home and abroad. Civil rights, anti-war, and black nationalist protests encompassed the sixties. The Civil Rights Movement, culminating with the Civil Rights Act (1964) and the Voting Rights Act (1965), resulted in equality under the law for blacks and other racial minorities. Protests against the Vietnam War revealed that it is disproportionately the poor and minorities in America who bleed in U.S. wars. The black nationalist movement turned racism on its head with shouts of "black is beautiful!"

Spurred by frustration at demands not met by the Civil Rights Movement, advocates of black separatism gained wide support thoughout the African American community in the late sixties and early seventies. Movement leaders, inspired by Malcolm X, adopted the name "black" in place of "Negro." Malcolm X clearly differentiated between the Negro who "apologizes for his black skin" and has a "begging attitude" and the proud black man who, rather than apologizing, sees himself as "part of the vast majority [of the world] who outnumber whites, and therefore [do not] have to beg the white man for anything" [1971:91,92]. Black nationalists demanded, rather than pleaded, for equal rights.

Black pride was evident in the coronation of Robin Gregory as homecoming queen at Howard University in 1967. Traditionally, homecoming queens at Howard were students who came close to epitomizing the European style and fashion of female beauty. Most were light-skinned, with straightened hair and European features. Robin Gregory was a black activist who wore her hair in an Afro. Her election as Howard's homecoming queen was a "pivotal point" in the history of the university. A student-led drive to transform Howard into a symbol of black pride broke forth at the coronation. Shouts of "Black Power!" spread throughout the packed auditorium as Gregory was revealed the winner of the homecoming queen election [Hampton and Fayer, 1990:435,436]. Blackness, rather than whiteness, became Howard's symbol of beauty.

While many other and varied assaults on authority and tradition took place after the Civil Rights Movement peaked, it was the successes of the Movement that encouraged the latter challenges to the status quo. The Civil Rights Movement was a watershed. The roots of the current transformation of black-white racial identity can be traced back to it. On the structural level, legislation was enacted during that era that encouraged the treatment and perception of blacks as equal to whites. Culturally, the turbulence and protests of the late fifties and sixties contributed to an atmosphere in which interracial marriages and their biracial offspring were increasingly accepted by mainstream white America.[14]

As the sixties progressed, and Civil Rights protests were both accompanied and then followed by the War on Poverty, the Vietnam War, widespread experimentation with drugs, and sexual liberation, Americans began to turn inward. They were forced to confront defeat in both the domestic and the foreign war and continual social upheaval at home. During the seventies, individualism and interest group politics were spawned. "The Black liberation movement, the women's movement, the lesbian and gay movements, and others that emerged in the fifties, sixties, and seventies were part of a new tradition that embraced an 'identity oriented paradigm'" [Schwerner, 1995]. Identity-focused politics engulfed U.S. culture. It was out of these movements that today's multiculturalism was born.

Prior to the existence of multiculturalism, there was little debate on how biracial persons should identify themselves. Black nationalists opposed interracial marriages.[15] Many perceived a black person marrying across the color line as a rejection of blackness. In turn many African Americans, embracing "black pride," maintained that the offspring of these parents should embrace their black heritage and identify with it completely. Meanwhile, whites continued to assume that if anyone had a black parent they were de facto black. Biracial Americans were racially defined by both blacks and whites as simply black.

Today, however, racial identity is neither so quickly nor so easily defined. Just as the protests of the sixties challenged tradition and encouraged interracial relationships, multiculturalism has encouraged the affirmation of all racial combinations. Noted psychologists and psychiatrists have come "to the opinion that for a person of mixed ancestry to neglect one or the other parent's identity [is] to detract from a clear racial identity." Biracial support groups "came into existence in the early 1980s on the explicit premise that both Black and non-Black identities [are] necessary to the well-being of both interracial marriages and their offspring" [Spickard, 1989:339]. The result is that biracial Americans no longer have an obvious racial identity.

Many older children of interracial marriages cling to the belief that, in our racially divided society, the only healthy way a biracial person can racially identify is as black. On the other hand, a growing number of younger biracial Americans are opting to recognize both sides of their racial heritage. The reasons behind and repercussions of this transformation in racial identity are the subject of the following chapters.

NOTES

1. The original story in Genesis 9 and 10 was that after the Flood, Ham had looked upon his father's nakedness as Noah lay drunk in his tent, but the other two sons, Shem and Japheth, had covered their father without looking upon him; when Noah awoke, he cursed Canaan, son of Ham, saying that he would be a 'servant of servants' unto his brothers" [Jordan, 1968:17]. Many Christian defenders of the concept of black slavery maintained that Noah's curse on Ham and his son Canaan resulted in all of their descendants being black. In turn, in the eyes of many pro-slavery Christians, dark skin became a sign of sinfulness, degradation, and slavery.

2. The only blacks who would have the freedom to choose to marry interracially.

3. Reuter calculates this figure by estimating with the few available figures of mixed-race persons during this period. He takes Maryland's stated number of black-white persons in 1755, estimates from that figure the total number of mixed-race persons in the colonies at that time (Maryland had approximately one-sixth the total African population), and then doubles the population due to a generation of natural growth by 1790. See Reuter, 1918/1969:112 for his direct explanation of the 60,000 figure.

4. Some organizations excluded potential members if their skin was darker than a brown paper bag. Likewise, some societies barred entrance to those who did not have prominent blue veins or could not pass a comb through their hair. In each case, attempts were made to exclude those who did not have prominent European features.

5. While Samuel Tilden had actually won the popular vote, a compromise was struck whereby the Democrats would accede to a Hayes victory and the Republicans would end Reconstruction and leave the former Confederate states to manage their own racial affairs.

6. Basically, this entailed former slaves sharecropping on land owned by former masters.

7. The idea that *any* black ancestry makes one black.

8. All plans for embarking on an exodus to Africa under the leadership of Garvey were effectively squelched when he was imprisoned in 1923 on charges of using the mails to defraud in his efforts to raise funds for his steamship line. He was pardoned by President Calvin Coolidge in 1927 and deported as an "undesirable alien" [Franklin, 1980:356].

9. "Jim Crow" is the term used to describe a system of segregation between whites and nonwhites in the United States. The system was given constitutional sanction in the 1896 *Plessy v. Ferguson* Supreme Court decision, which declared that "separate but equal" facilities for blacks and whites was constitutional. This case stems from the attempt of Plessy, who was seven-eighths Caucasian and one-eighth African to gain the privileges of white Americans. Interestingly, he maintained that, because his African heritage was not discernible, he should have the same rights as any white man. The Court ignored this argument of Plessy's and concentrated on whether or not enforced separation of whites and nonwhites was a violation of the Thirteenth and Fourteenth Amendments. They deemed that it was not. In their decision they declared the validity of Jim Crow legislation and the "one drop rule." It was not until 1954 with the *Brown v. Board of Education* decision that this verdict was overturned in the public school systems. It was not until 1964 and 1965 with the Civil Rights Acts and the Voting Rights Act that African Americans were given equal rights under U.S. laws.

10. W.E.B. Du Bois used this term to refer to the finest and brightest of the African American population of his time period.

11. While Reuter's numbers are debatable (there has never been any accurate designation of exactly how many black Americans are of mixed-race descent), it is certainly evident that the majority of the most eminent African Americans in U.S. history had white forebearers. There are a multitude of reasons why the chances for mixed-race persons of achieving success in society were so much greater than for "pure" African Americans. Most white Americans, and many blacks as well, viewed African Americans with white features, such as light skin, thin nose and lips, more favorably than those with more traditional African features. In turn, they were treated with more respect from both communities. The few opportunities that were available for black Americans went primarily to those who looked the "whitest." Leadership positions, business backing, and schooling were more likely to be available for light-skinned than dark-skinned blacks. This, in turn, led to the natural educational, business, and leadership ascension of mixed-race persons in the black community.

12. Before this time, different variations of mixed-race categories were included. All categories were to be filled on the basis of the judgment of the census taker, relying on his or her visual perception [Davis, 1991:11,12].

13. While a large majority of these couple are black male and white female, there are some indications that the percentage of black female and white male marriages is increasing.

14. This increasing level of acceptance did not extend to some areas of the black

community. Black nationalist groups emphasized black pride and self-sufficiency and opposed interracial unions.

15. This was especially true for black women marrying white men. They were seen as cavorting with the "master." Black men who married white women, on the other hand, were often seen in a more forgiving light because they were coupling with a member of another oppressed group—white females. Of course, this lent itself to providing cover for many black males who appreciated white women more as a symbol of ideal beauty than as partners in oppression. One result of these stricter racial standards for black females was the fact that they were left with fewer potential marriageable partners.

2

"Black by Definition" or "The Best of Both Worlds?"

Each age cohort views the world from a unique perspective. The events of their lifetime shape their outlook on society. For instance, the prevailing ideology of the 1950s convinced the majority of Americans who came of age during that decade to believe that a woman's place is in the home. Many of those who grew up a mere three decades later, however, would scoff at the notion that females were born to be homemakers. A somewhat similar change in the racial identification of mixed-race persons took place during the three decades between the mid-1960s and the mid-1990s. Findings from the present study indicate that both young biracial adults and young Americans in general are now more likely to identify someone with both a black and a white parent as biracial than as black. This is a dramatic difference from the way the previous generation of Americans racially defined children of interracial couples.

In order to understand this transformation, it is helpful to hear the stories of biracial adults who were born before, during, and after the Civil Rights Movement. The case studies presented in this chapter focus on three biracial persons whose lives span these time periods: Susan spent her childhood in the fifties; Chris was a preteen during the Movement era of the sixties; and Rasheed grew up during the Reagan and Bush presidencies.

All three interviewees give compelling testimony as to how the society in which they were raised influenced their racial identity. In order to give some organization to their stories, each case study covers four topics: (1) formative years: early schooling, friendships, and how race was discussed in the home; (2) life, race, and romance: influence of race in overall life and, in particular, romantic relationships; (3) society's racial lens, racial categories, and racial self-definition: society's racial perception, forms with racial classifications, and racial self-definition; and (4) being biracial: positive or negative?: whether being biracial has been more of a positive or a negative experience.

GROWING UP BEFORE THE MOVEMENT

Susan

I don't think that there's such a thing as a biracial person. . . . I think a person who has African heritage is African American, whether they're biracial culturally or not. The theory of race as it's used in this culture does not allow for anything else.

Susan, forty-six, had an African American father and a white mother. Her parents met after her father, disgusted and stymied by rampant discrimination in America, went to an East African nation to take a job as a schoolteacher. There he met his wife who, while descending from a mixture of Greek and East African aristocracy, appears white.

When Susan was seven, the family returned to America because of her father's various health ailments. They settled in a small suburban town in California. An African American widow agreed to sell them her house. Their father had chosen this predominantly white town because he believed a white, middle-class neighborhood would come equipped with a good public school system for his children.

Once in the United States, Susan confronted a hostile society. During the pre-Civil Rights era of the 1950s, racial mixing was not common. Residential neighborhoods were carefully segregated throughout the United States. Black Americans who dared to live in a white neighborhood were often not tolerated by their white neighbors. Redlining[1] made it difficult, if not impossible, for residential integration to occur. When it did happen, white neighbors often did all they could to insure that other blacks would not follow. One common means of trying to prevent a further influx of African Americans was to make the new black family feel as unwelcome as possible. In many instances cross burnings, rock throwings, and other types of physical violence were utilized by the white residents.

While Susan's family avoided physical intimidation, they were confronted with much psychological oppression in their neighborhood. The discrimination they faced from white people worked to strengthen their sense of belonging to the black world. Susan racially defines herself as African American. The fact that she is a member of the age cohort that grew up in the 1950s and 1960s strongly influenced her racial self-definition.

Formative Years

So, here we were, this black family moving into this white community. There had been another black family that had lived in, the house we lived in and they moved. So we moved into this house and got a lot of subtle and not so subtle hints that we weren't really welcome. Initially, my parents tried to put me in a Catholic school. And the local Catholic priest said, "Sorry, we don't take your kind." A couple of neighbors who lived a couple of houses up came over. They were Catholic and very big contributors of that Church and they asked, "Gee, why don't you put your daughter in a Catholic school?" My parents said, "We tried and there's the response we got." And they went back to the priest and said, "Either you change that or we're leaving the Church." And he changed it; but in the meantime my parents had said, "Why would we send our daughter to a school where she is not wanted?" So they put me in this public school that was right around the corner from where I lived.

In my neighborhood, there were two Japanese families, one Chinese family. Their kids and I became friends. We had to become friends. What were the choices there? And it wasn't that other people weren't polite sometimes. Some were, some weren't, some were vicious. But, clearly, we were who each other had. We had some things in common, not a lot. Looking back, really not a lot. When I reached junior high school, I became friends with another girl who was an absolute rebel. And she and I became best friends. She was European American. And even my friendship with her had its limitations. Places that it just couldn't go.

One example of these limitations was her sixteenth birthday. We planned it together and were really excited about it. Her birthday was right before mine. And then as we were getting ready to make it all happen, her parents said to her that she could not invite me. And it turned out that the reason why was that parents of other kids who had been invited said, "Our kids can't come if she's there." And so they had to make a choice. Either let their kid have a sixteenth birthday party and not invite me or invite me and understand there wasn't going to be a sixteenth birthday party. It was that clear.

What was also clear was that Susan faced all the prejudice and discrimination any black girl would have encountered growing up in that neighborhood. Her father realized this and prepared her and her brother for this reality. He taught them that they were black and would be treated as such by their white neighbors.

I think my father's family felt some concern about us living in the 'burbs, about the kind of message that sent us. My father made sure we knew, always knew that we were black. And then it was you were Negro, then you got to be black, and now we get to be African American, whatever. But that was our cultural identity.

Life, Race, and Romance

The impact Susan's blackness had on her life in this white-dominated society was tremendous. Looking back, she realizes it has affected every aspect of her life. As a child and young woman, Susan's racial background prevented her from participating in many typical youth activities, from being a Blue Bird to dating.

I tried to join the Blue Birds. I wanted to be a Blue Bird. And my next-door neighbor was the Blue Bird leader, and when I showed up, she told me at the front door, "We don't take your kind." I was eight years old at the time. Eight and a half. Something like that. So I ended up becoming a girl scout. My girl scout troop leader was the mother of one of the Asian American kids I hung out with.

Another time, my parents tried to enroll me in a group, in an organization called Jacks and Jills that still exists for African American kids. My parents wanted to enroll me, and they were basically told, "Oh if the mother's white, there's not a chance." Not quite in those words, but basically.

I dated primarily European American men. That's been my context. That's where I grew up. Although I think I've made the choice at this point in my life, that's not something

I want to do anymore. I don't think I fit in a relationship with a European American man. There are just too many complications, too much time having to explain myself.

It took a long time for me to understand the implications of who I was in this culture. I remember sitting in college, my freshman year in college, when I was in California still, and having a white guy that I'd grown up with sitting across a table from me. He and I were playing cards at the time at lunch. Somebody at the table had said something about dating, and then they got up and left the table. And I said, "You know, it's funny, I never dated. I never dated. Never dated. Never had a date in high school, junior high, none of that sort of stuff." And he said, "Well, lots of people wanted to ask you out." And I said, "What do you mean?" And he said, "Our parents made sure we understood that we could never ask you out."

I remember one guy calling me up one time. You know, we were having a conversation. And when I told somebody he'd called, I never heard from him again. And he actually avoided me for a lot of years. And I remember a new guy coming to town. And I thought he was the cutest guy, and he played baseball. He was on the baseball team [laughing]. It's so silly now [laughing]. But it was real then. And having him ask me to hold his books during the game and giving me his watch and stuff. And his house was on the way back to my house. And walking back to his house and giving him all his books and realizing when I got home that I still had his watch on my wrist and I needed to give it back right then. And going back and having his parents, one of his parents, answer the door, giving him the watch back. And from then on he didn't speak to me. He never spoke to me again. From that day, it must have been seventh or eighth grade, from then on until we graduated high school he never spoke to me again.

Having those kinds of really weird experiences and then having them all tied back for me made me start to understand the implications of who I am in this culture. A few people's comments later about, "Well, we couldn't invite you out" or "We couldn't do that." So. . . I always felt safest in the black community, to some degree. I felt cared for to some degree. Although, again, at a distance.

Society's Racial Lens, Racial Categories, and Racial Self-Definition

While different in many ways, Susan and her mother share light skin coloring. Because Susan appears white to most people, yet self-identifies as black, she has had to proclaim her blackness repeatedly throughout her life. It has also made her privy to white disdain for blacks in a way that most blacks are not.

I know that initially, when I walk into an African American setting, there's always some sense of suspicion about me. You know, "Who the hell is she and why is she here?" I actually did a workshop about two and a half years ago. I was asked to lead a part of this conference for half a day. And it never even dawned on me. It's so much a part of my identity, so much a part of me, that it didn't dawn on me until probably an hour and a half into this process that the glares I was getting from some of these folks were because they thought I was a white woman leading this conference of African Americans. And they were not happy [laughs]. And I finally thought, "Oh my God, I've got to make some self-identifying comments in here." And I try to do that all the time, because I know it's really hard for a lot of African Americans to look at me and say, "Who the hell are you? Why are you here? What are you doing with us?"

On the other hand, I know that I spent so much of my life in and among white America, as opposed to in and among black America, that I hear things and see things that would normally never be said or done in the presence of someone who's skin was darker than mine. And I am conscious of the depth of the fear and loathing that exists in white America in ways that other African Americans are not. Even now in this institutional setting at times I work with someone, a congregation group or a different type of group, and they will have no idea who I am in terms of my racial identity. And they'll say stuff that just makes me sick. Just makes me absolutely sick. And I know it doesn't matter that it's in this setting because I've been in too many. I've been in the banking world. I've been in the legal world. I've been in too many other places where I know that's not what it's about.

Despite her own skin color, Susan does not believe that there is a biracial racial category. In fact, she maintains that it is wrong to encourage young adults with both a black and a white parent to identify as anything other than black. According to Susan, the bottom line is that they will always be identified as black and they should be prepared for that.

I've worked with a lot of young people who are in their twenties and thirties now, who have struggled with the identity of being biracial and not one race. See, there is a question of why they don't want to be black. Because they understand that there are power and privilege issues connected to who they choose to be. And the culture says, if you're black, you are connected somehow to welfare, and you're connected somehow with crime, and you're connected somehow with all these bad things, not with the economic survival of America, which is the truth [slight laugh]. And so they don't want to be that. And yet, [they have to deal with being perceived as black] when they apply for a job, when they go to college, when they are at home with their parents, if they're dark-skinned and they have a light-skinned parent, a mother or father, and they walk down the street, the lack of recognition that they are parent and child. Just so many things that they will have to deal with because society will view them as black.

One young man—his coloring is probably like mine—was telling me about his sister and he walking down the street together—his sister is a little darker. They were on a college campus, and people stopped him afterwards and asked, "What are you doing with that black woman? You can get any woman you want. What are you doing with her?" And he said, "That's my sister." The pain of that, of having to make those choices is enormous. Much of it depends on family grounding. Much of that depends on the parents making the decision early on that they are going to be a black family, not trying to pull this biracial stuff. It's a nice term. It's interesting. But in the politic of our society, it counts for nothing.

I don't think that there's such a thing as a biracial person [laughs]. I mean, I think there is such a thing as a biracial family and a biracial individual. But I think a person who has African heritage is African American, whether they're biracial culturally or not. The theory of race as it's used in this culture does not allow for anything else.

I self-identify as an African American woman—always will—because I know when I apply for a job, when I walk down a street, when I do whatever else, nobody cares about anything other than the fact that my father was African American. The rest of it is sort of trivial and interesting. But that's the basic criteria by which I will always be judged. As will my brother.

Being Biracial: Positive or Negative?

Susan believes that society disparages her blackness and does not recognize her white racial background. Having a black parent and a white foreign parent has made her life difficult.

Being biracial has been a real challenging experience, a perpetual feeling of not necessarily belonging in any one place. Other than my brother, I never felt a real sense of connection to family. And, you know, he and I didn't get along for a long time— probably till we started living apart [laughs]. But that's normal sibling stuff, you know. And I think he and I have come to kind of explore some of the similarities in how we came out of where we grew up. But our lives have been very different. We've made very different choices. It's taken me a long time to really understand the depth of the effect on me of my being biracial, that many of the things that have happened to me—the jobs where I've not gotten the promotions I needed to have and could have had and should have had, the people whom I dated who never took our relationship beyond a certain point—that all of this had to do with race. It took a long time for me to understand it.

GROWING UP DURING THE MOVEMENT

Chris

I identify as, and this is not in order of importance, as black and biracial. . . . My parents, though, racially identified me as black. . . . It's a generational thing to some degree. Within this country, anyone who had any kind of drop of black blood was automatically assumed to be black. And we grew up with that understanding. . . . It was very clear.

Chris was raised in New York City by his white Jewish mother and his black father. His parents met in the late 1940s while they both worked behind the scenes at a New York City theater. He and his older sister grew up middle class: his mother worked as a financial analyst for the state, and his father worked a variety of jobs. Born in 1958, almost a decade after Susan's birth, his racial identity is tinged with the effects of the Civil Rights Movement. As Susan was, he and his sister were racially designated as black as they grew up. However, while firmly declining to identify as white, Chris maintains that he is both black and biracial. Unlike Susan, he believes he would be "missing out" if he chose to identify only as black. Presently, Chris works as a social worker on a college campus. He formed and runs a support group for mixed-race students.

Formative Years

The apartment building I grew up in was predominantly Irish Catholic. There were two issues in that particular neighborhood with the kids I associated with. One, that we were Jewish, and two, that we were black. And that didn't go over too well. I remember one incident when I was about twelve where I got into a fight with a kid over something like winning bases or something like that. And he called me a nigger. I got into a fight with him and wrestled him to the ground. I was not into beating him into a pulp, but I just got him to "surrender," for lack of a better description.

I went back to my parents where my sister and my mother happened to be around and told them what happened. My sister went down and basically threatened to kill anybody. . . . Well, she made it clear in her own way that any other comment like that would warrant a quick and immediate response. And she was the kind of person you wouldn't mess with.

Growing up in a neighborhood where there was some hostility directed at my particular ethnicities made me pretty pleased about who I was, because I wasn't too fond of the people who didn't like me. I figured if I didn't like them and they didn't like me cause of this, there must be something good about me.

Even outside the neighborhood, in a private school, Chris had to deal with racism. There he had to handle discrimination from teachers as well as students. He remembers, in particular, how one teacher blatantly mistreated him and the one other student of color in the class.

In the third grade there was myself and another black kid, her name was Merideth. This one teacher, I can't remember her name, used to send me and Merideth out with the teaching assistant to go play all the time. We thought we were getting ahead of everybody else. But, obviously, she didn't want us in the class. So she had us playing in the playground when she was teaching the lesson.

So that was interesting. In that case, I mean, of course I wasn't going to tell my parents because they thought I ought to be in class. But I remember the teacher reprimanding me because my father taught me how to write my name in script. She said, "Never do that in here." And I remember her sending us out a lot. This was the mid to late sixties when that happened.

Life, Race, and Romance

As a young adult, Chris experienced racial prejudice and discrimination at college. He attended a large, predominantly white university in the Midwest. He wonders now how he was able to deal with some of the racism he encountered there.

I think my first big exposure to institutional racism was at college. That school was not open to students of color. They were looking at just satisfying the federal requirements in any way, shape, or form and to hell with it. I knew enough to request the best housing because I had gone to summer school at the college before my freshman year. Most of the other students of color, not knowing the campus, were simply assigned where to live. Eighty-five percent of the students of color were all in this really crappy area dorm. And I remember asking my house head about it once. This was always a sensitive subject in that house. And he said that "he didn't know why, but he figured the school probably thought they were more used to that kind of environment." The only reason why I was in that dorm was because I knew what dorm to ask for because I'd been at the college the summer before. But that was interesting to witness. Kind of like being in unfriendly waters on occasion is a nice way of putting it.

I wonder why I didn't kill my roommate when I was in those waters. I found out that he used to refer to me as the "houseboy." And my anger might be directed at him, but also the fact that no one in that dorm ever said anything to him, with the exception of somebody's girlfriend, who didn't live in the dorm. Everybody else kind of kept it quiet. Would I have had that experience had I been in a more racially mixed or dorm predominantly of color? I don't know. But frankly, I think my sense of self and who I am has certainly been strengthened by having those kinds of experiences. Much like for my father. I think such experiences really had an effect on his life. I also think it really strengthened him. My background and my life experiences, I think, strengthened my sister and myself as well. I'd say we're pretty well rooted and reasonably sane.

Chris's experience of white racism did not lead him to spurn relationships with white persons. He has a racially diverse group of friends and did not prefer to date one race of women over another. Race has, though, been a factor in some of his romantic relationships.

I think whomever wanted to date me I'd date at one point [laughing]. I never chose not to date someone because of their race. Race was not a big factor. I would say that in some cases with people I've met race was a big factor. There were some who may have wanted to date only someone of their same race. Or because someone may have seen me as being sort of an exotic kind of figure. It was weird. I mean there was a white friend of my wife's whom I met and immediately took a dislike to. We refer to her as being "liberal," which in my life is not exactly the best term to use. She is the type of person a black man, not worried about ethics, could have used for sex, because she was trying to prove something. It was interesting. I met a lot of people like that. . . . But no, I never made that judgment.

One relationship that comes to mind in which my being biracial was an issue was with a woman with whom I was together for about five years. And I think the issue of race. . . in that particular case, I think there were three different factors in it: religion, race, and region. I don't think they liked the fact that I was from New York. In the five years that I was with this particular woman, I never met her parents, though her mother was very pleasant when we broke up briefly. I think they were very relieved when we stopped dating.

She was white and Protestant. She caused a major scandal [with her family] when she lived with me briefly. I expect they're much happier with whoever she happens to be with now. Then again, she probably could have gone off and brought home a woman and they would have been happier. I used to joke and stuff with friends that "If your parents don't like who you're dating, bring me over and they'll like anything." And that's just part of the nature of things.

Chris left the dating world over three years ago when he married a white woman. Both his mother and his wife's parents were relieved that their child married a Jew. Race remains an inescapable issue, however.

My mother was quite relieved because she's Jewish. That was the big one. I think her family was relieved based on that . . . I know the issue of race has been a concern for her parents. And we've talked about it. Obviously that's something that comes up and we think it important to discuss . . . I think she is seeing more, she is witnessing more than I think she would want to witness. It's unfortunate for her, it comes with "the baggage," so to speak.

Not too long ago, my wife and I happened to be in a store and I was being followed by a security guard. I understood what the dynamics were, and I had to deal with this. My wife on the other hand wanted to pound them shitless. And we had to process that experience because this was her first real dealing with someone whom she loved having that experience.

Society's Racial Lens, Racial Categories, and Racial Self-Definition

While Chris has been "mistaken for many things," he has never been perceived as white. Because of his tightly curled hair and light brown complexion, Chris has had to deal with both racial misperceptions and prejudices. He has little patience for those who judge him simply by his appearance. Chris's racial self-definition parallels the societal transformation occurring during his lifetime. Following the pre-Movement "one drop rule," his parents defined him as black. A product of the seventies, himself, Chris describes himself as both black and biracial.

There have been times when I think people have issues with my being biracial. African Americans, just as whites. I don't know if it's based on my background, as much as the color of my skin. I mean, there's the issue of colorism, which I think is just a parallel to the issue of race within the country. Frankly, my attitude has been I don't have time. Growing up I didn't have time to care about the color of someone's skin. Now, as I'm getting older I have less tolerance. So, if someone has an issue with it, they can screw themselves. It's not something that you enjoy. I'm really not too fond of having someone judge me about my color, but that's been something that's gone on.

Like with anything else, I feel I have a variety of racial identifications. In the generational sense I only go back one generation becaues I think it would be too confusing for myself and everybody else. I identify as, and this is not in order of importance, as black and biracial. If I only focused on one without the other, I would be missing out on a few things.

I don't identify as being white. Understanding this is more of a political statement on my part. I believe for someone to be white they have certain privileges which I am not privy to. Therefore, I do not identify with that.

It's a generational thing to some degree. Within this country anyone who had a drop of black blood was automatically assumed to be black. And we grew up with that understanding. While we were biracial, I don't think we used that term. I don't know what term we used at that point. I don't think that "biracial" was being used. I certainly didn't like the term "mulatto." I always found that to be offensive. We were black. But we also had parents of two different races. My parents, though, racially identified me as black. No question about that. I think that was also, again, how they grew up. It was very clear.

Being Biracial: Positive or Negative?

I am very happy with who I am. I wouldn't trade it. What I've been exposed to—both good and bad—has made me a better person. While I can't say how different I would be if I was monoracial, being biracial and being exposed to a variety of things has definitely been a plus for me. I don't think I have nearly as much baggage on a lot of things as a lot of monoracial people do. I also may probably be externalizing it, saying it's more their problem than mine, which makes things a lot easier.

GROWING UP AFTER THE MOVEMENT

Rasheed

I think in the future we're not going to have the race question on the Census anymore, because it's not going to matter anyway. . . . Some people say that America is not the melting pot people say it is, but I think it is . . . There are very few one hundred percent Hispanics, as there are very few one hundred percent African Americans, as there are . . . It's mixing. It's going to mix.

Rasheed is an eighteen-year-old college student. Race has not played a large role in Rasheed's life. It was not a topic of discussion in his household. He tends to brush off the few negative racial incidents he has experienced.

Rasheed was raised in a middle-class household with various siblings and half-siblings by his mother. His mother is white and his father is black; they never married, though Rasheed's father still plays an active role in his life. Rasheed himself is perceived by most people as black.

Formative Years

I'm eighteen. I was born in upstate New York. And that's pretty much where I lived until now. My mother's Caucasian, my father's African, or black, whatever. They were never married. My mother was married, so I have siblings and half-siblings. I'm closer to my mother's side, since I live with my mother. I never met my father's parents because they died before I was born. When my dad used to live in the city where I live, I'd see him very frequently. Then he moved to Nevada. But I still talk to him often. He comes up summers and was at my graduation, all the important dates he comes up.

My mother was an administrative assistant or something like that. She worked for a Presbyterian church. My father, I don't know. He used to work, I think, at Union Carbide. But what he was doing there I don't know [laughs]. I'd say we were middle class when I was growing up.

When I was up to five, my neighborhood was more racially even, but I think it's a little bit more white now. And where I lived after that, it's pretty much all white. Most of my friends have been white. I do have some black friends and some Spanish friends. But most of them are white. I went to a magnet school. Magnet schools were created to integrate the schools. These magnet schools were supposed to have all the high tech and the best things, so people would be bused in. So my elementary school, which was kindergarten through eighth grade, was pretty much racially half and half, it was all mixed. So, actually, a lot of my friends were of diverse races. They were all bused and I didn't live near them, but they were my friends at school. And being young, you didn't ask for phone numbers then. So back then all my friends were pretty much of all races, it didn't really matter. Everybody was like half and half. But in high school, I think my school might have been a bit more Hispanic and black. Those were like the three: Hispanic, white, and black. And I think it was a bit more black and Hispanic than white. But my closest friends are white or Hispanic, pretty much. I just have more in common with them really.

It's really weird, I don't think about stuff like this until people ask questions. I just don't think about race. I just like people by their interests. Like I was in art, and my best friend Dan, he was in art, too. So, we got really close there. He and my other best friend,

Jan—they're both white. There weren't a lot of black students in art. There were a few. Like my friend Ben, he's black, and he was in art. It was a four-year high school and we had majors, somewhat. And there were pretty much two art classes in this major of my graduating class. And some years there would be more black kids, but most of the time there were more white kids in my class. It just happened with people's schedules, that's the way it happened, and in my other major, Aquatic Ecology, there were also a lot of white students.

At home we never really talked much about the fact that my father is black and my mother is white. It was just kind of there, that's what I am. My parents and I didn't talk about it much. Well, I did ask my mom—I don't know why, just when I was little, just like, you know, "am I German or Irish, or whatever?"—so I asked my mom, and my mother told me what my father was. I was just wondering. I don't remember why I asked that then. I think she also explained it's Africa, somewhere, but they really don't know where because of slavery. I guess I was old enough to understand that, like fourth grade. Maybe second or first grade was the first time I asked, and it wasn't that in-depth of an explanation. It was just, "You're father's black and I'm German and English." It was, I think, because we were talking about Native Americans in class. We were doing the pioneers and the Pilgrims and stuff. And the teacher asked who was a Native American in the class. So I was just wondering. I think I did ask my mother, "Am I a Native American at all or anything?" Cause I was just curious, cause I thought that was really cool that those kids were Native Americans. Like, they were part of the Pilgrims and the Indians and everything. That was the first time I asked. The fact that my father's black and my mother's white was never an issue with anyone when I was growing up. They never voiced it if it was, and I never felt anything from anybody.

Life, Race, and Romance

Rasheed's racial background played so small a role in his childhood, he hardly thinks of it, even today. He can think of only one instance in which he may have experienced discrimination due to his race. Race in general is not a focus of Rasheed's attention.

It's weird, I don't really think about race. When I'm describing somebody to somebody, I really seldom say that. If it's brought up in class like February, black history month, I think about it a little bit more. And Martin Luther King, Jr. day I think about race a little bit more. Then just little things come in like when I'm describing somebody, I'm thinking to myself, "Wow, I didn't tell them if they were white or black."

Have I been discriminated against because of the way people perceive of me racially? It's never been very forward if it has happened. Here's an example. I was younger than I am now, though not much. If I went in a store, once in a while I'd notice like this one person who was probably the store security person. I'd keep running into him, as if he was following me. But ,t could be just a coincidence that I'm just running into him, so I really didn't think much about it. But, other than that, no, I never really experienced discrimination openly.

Even in dating, race has not been a major issue for Rasheed. He does not believe race will play a factor in whom he decides to marry. However, he is most often attracted to women with Caucasian features.

Both my girlfriends have been white. I've found some very beautiful black girls. Although hair is kind of important, I like curly hair. I like more natural looking hair. Like if a girl's got a lot of hair spray or gel in it, I don't like that. Also I don't like it when some black girls put a little grease in their hair. But I like Hispanic or Puerto Rican women. That or usually white. Race has never come up. It's never like, "Oh, you're black" or that my father is.

Race wouldn't matter to me when it comes to whom I might eventually settle down with. But it's interesting, most of the girls I like have long, curly hair, are shorter than I am, and have little, petite features, like nice little noses. All those are characteristics of whites or Hispanics.

Society's Racial Lens, Racial Categories, and Racial Self-Definition

I think society thinks I'm black. I think just because of the color of my skin, what they see first is what they think. I think after they get to know me they question it. Or some people even come up to me and ask me if I'm Hispanic, or actually, in school, they just come up and start speaking Spanish to me, thinking I'm Puerto Rican or whatever. And my sister who's also mixed, she's lighter than I am. And actually one of her friend's mothers thought she was Italian.

On my SATs and my college papers I put down black. When I was in school, I don't know exactly what my racial category was. I guess school records in elementary school have to put you down as something. My mother knew a lot of people at my elementary school. So, I think there it was like whichever you need a number for [laughs], that was that. Most of the time I think I put down black or just didn't color it in at all. Sometimes, every once in a while I'd put white or "other." Sometimes, "other" did not mean mixed racial, so I just wanted to make sure. And sometimes I put down white. Most of the time I think I put down black, though. I was like, "Let's see if I can mess up your records now" [laughs].

Honestly speaking, I put down black for the SATs and college applications because I knew some colleges would have like affirmative action, or whatever. Although I knew I could get in on my grades, every little bit helps. They always say "give yourself something to make yourself stand out." So I wrote a great essay, I thought. I think my grades were good. SATs could have been better, compared to college standards, but I think they were good. I'm not good at taking timed tests, so there's nothing I could really do about that. So I also wrote down that I was black. A combination of things. Whether they considered it or not, I don't know. None of the schools I applied to said they gave scholarships to minorities.

I think in the future we're not going to have the race question on the Census anymore, because it's not going to matter anyway. Like affirmative action is not going to matter. It's not going to matter what number you have in your class either way. I don't know, some people say that America is not the melting pot people say it is, but I think it is. It's like there are very few one hundred percent Hispanics, as there are very few one hundred percent African Americans, as there are . . . It's mixing. It's going to mix.

I don't really pick one race over the other. But as I was growing up, you know, like little black boys use slang and they play basketball and I suck at that. If you're going to take stereotypes, I suck at basketball, and slang just kind of goes over my head. I'm like "what?" [laughs]. But if someone asks me what my race is, I'd say both. I would say Caucasian and African American.

Being Biracial: Positive or Negative?

Rasheed believes that his racial background has been a positive influence on his life. He has been able to embrace both sides of his racial heritage. In turn, he looks upon himself as the beneficiary of the best of both the black and white worlds.

> I think, overall, being biracial has been more of a positive than a negative in my life. I get the best of both worlds. It's like, I don't remember what the comment was, but this girl asked me about something, it was pretty much two stereotypes. It was like what the white men were bad in, the black men were good in, but they were bad at what the white men were good in. She asked me, "What one are you like?" I said, "I got the best of both worlds [laughs]. I got both of the good parts." She was like, "do you have both of the bad parts?" I was like, "No, I've got the best of both worlds" [laughing].

CONCLUSION

As illustrated by these case studies, there has been a transformation in how biracial persons racially identify themselves. Biracial adults raised after the Civil Rights era are much less likely to consider themselves to be black than are mixed-race persons over the age of thirty. The most obvious reason for this change in racial identity is the matter of choice. Susan is clear in her understanding that, when she was growing up, her racial identity was determined for her by society. The choice was not hers to make—society deemed that she was black, period. Chris realizes that it is a "generational thing." His parents followed the "one drop rule" and identified him as black. Chris, on the other hand, while refusing to identify as white because he is not "privy to" the privileges of white society, does define himself as both black and biracial. Finally, Rasheed believes he is free to identify racially as both black and white.

The racial identities of the three persons presented in the case studies are consistent with the majority of the interviewees used in this research. Two-thirds of the biracial persons over the age of thirty self-identify as exclusively black, while less than one-third of the mixed-race persons under the age of thirty racially identify as black. Why this transformation has occurred is the focus of the next chapter.

NOTE

1. A discriminatory housing practice in which certain residential areas are put "off-limits" to prospective home buyers who are racial/ethnic minorities. Although it is now illegal, such discrimination still exists to varying extents throughout the United States.

3

The Transformation: From Black to Biracial

As the case studies in Chapter 2 illustrate, biracial persons born after the Civil Rights Movement are much more likely to identify as biracial than are those born before the Movement. A full two-thirds of this younger cohort feel free to recognize both sides of their racial heritage. However, as Anselm Strauss states in *Mirrors and Masks,* "the naming or identifying of things is . . . a continual problem, never really over and done with" [1959:25]. As seen in Chapter 1, biracial persons have been identified in numerous ways throughout U.S. history. The "one drop rule," while the most famous means of identifying Americans with any African heritage, has not been the constant method of racial demarcation in this nation. More ambiguous and sometimes contradictory rulings have been used at various times throughout the course of colonial and U.S. history. Today the racial identification of mixed-race persons is once again in flux.

A transformation in racial identity occurs when a change transpires in the manner in which persons are racially defined on both societal and individual levels. The process entails an objective and subjective shifting of racial definitions. Over the last three decades, there has been a gradual mutation in how biracial persons have been "named" in our society. Strauss declares, "it is not change that needs to be explained but its specific directions" [1959:43]. The importance of change derives from the nature and consequences of the alteration. Why this current transformation of black/white mixed-race identity involves a movement from black to biracial is examined in this chapter.

A study of any social process concerning race must include a consideration of contexts [Lal, 1995]. Historical, cultural, and immediate social settings (e.g., family, peers, social class) are key factors in any research concerning race and identity. All three contexts influence the formation of personal and collective identity. There is an ongoing dialectic between individual persons and their families and the larger society. It is in the immediate social environment that the influences of history and culture take effect on the individual. History and culture, in turn, are formed by the collective and distinct actions of individuals.

Throughout all historical, cultural, and social settings, racial appearance has been of paramount importance in racial identification. Physical features play a major role in determining identity and social categories. Therefore, when examining racial identity, appearance must also be taken into account.

This chapter examines the various, often interrelated, influences of history, culture, immediate social setting, and racial appearance on the transformation of racial identity among biracial persons.[1] While covering these factors independently is an artificial separation of variables that are closely intertwined, it is necessary to examine them in this way in order to relate accurately their collective influence on the transformation. The chapter concludes with an examination of how these four influences affect both each other and the very existence of racial classifications in the United States.

THE CONTINUAL INFLUENCE OF RACIAL APPEARANCE

Racial appearance has always influenced the racial self-definition of biracial Americans. Throughout history, those mixed-race people who appear white have had the option of "passing." In light of this possibility, in years past, white society was constantly fearful of "invisible blacks." Many white Americans were concerned that they might accidentally socially mix with a person who, while appearing white, was "really" black and thus irreparably harm their good standing in society. A biracial person "becoming" white, however, entailed tremendous personal costs. In order to pass successfully into the white race, the biracial person had to make sure that he or she would never be exposed by a black acquaintance, friend, or family member. All ties to the black side of their families had to be cut.

Today, with equality under the law, there is much less incentive for biracial people to "become" white. While stories still exist of some doing so, the numbers of those who do have certainly decreased since the heyday of "passing" during the Jim Crow era. However, even if one does not choose to "pass," being perceived as white, or at least nonblack, does affect the racial identity of biracial Americans. Now that the "one drop rule" is no longer universally adhered to, the significance of racial appearance on racial identity among biracial persons has increased tremendously.

Racial appearance is much more likely to influence the racial self-definition of biracial persons born after the Civil Rights era than those born before the Movement. Biracial persons over thirty usually identify racially as black, no matter what their racial appearance. Of the sixty-two persons interviewed, fifteen appear white.[2] Seven are under the age of thirty and eight are older than thirty. While only one of those eight interviewees over the age of thirty identifies as biracial and the other seven define themselves as black, all seven of those under thirty identify as both black and white.

While today it is highly probable that young biracial persons who appear white will self-identify as both black and white, racial appearance has always been a factor in the racial perception of biracial persons by the general public. Biracial persons who do not look black have often been assumed by those who are not familiar with them to be white. With greater social mobility, and growing numbers of people living in large urban areas, racial appearance is increasingly important in how biracial individuals will be racially perceived. For instance, although she appears white, when Susan was growing up in her suburban town, she was known as black by all those who lived in that town. It was not until she moved out of that area that she came to be perceived as white by many people she encountered. Many of the under-thirty interviewees were raised in areas in which their family was not known to everyone in their town or city. Those who appear white, therefore, experienced being treated as a "white" person by many people with whom they interacted casually as they were growing up.

Today, as illustrated in her case study, Susan is often assumed to be a white woman by people who do not know her. This can result in some awkward situations. As mentioned in Chapter 2, she recalls leading a workshop for black women and suddenly realizing an hour or so into the program that her audience of African American women perceived her as white.

It didn't dawn on me until probably an hour and a half into this process that the glares I was getting from some of these folks were because they thought that I was a white woman leading this conference of African Americans. And they were not happy [laughs]. And I finally thought, "Oh my God, I've got to make some self-identifying comments in here." And I try to do that, all the time, because I know it's really hard for a lot of African Americans to look at me and say, "Who the hell are you? Why are you here? What are you doing with us?" [Susan, 46, perceived as white]

We all make "certain assumptions as to what the individual before us ought to be" [Goffman, 1963:2]. First appearances indicate that Susan is white, because of her light complexion. As Goffman would describe it, her "virtual social identity" is white. As Susan finally made it clear to the confused audience at the conference, her actual social identity is black. In just moments, in the minds of those seated before her, Susan had passed from an outsider to an in-group member. With the announcement of her identity as an African American woman, the tension dissipated and Susan gained acceptance from her audience.

Susan is not alone in being racially categorized merely on the basis of her appearance. Shawna, a twenty-year-old, describes how she and her friend, both biracial, are assumed to be different races by the general public.

With mixed people, people just look at you and say "you're black," "you're white," you know. If me and my friend Stacy are sitting next to each other, they're going to say I'm black and she's white. And we're both exactly the same. Her mother's white, my mother's white. Her mother's blonde, my mother's blonde. Her father's black and mine's black. We're the same thing, but somebody's going to say she's white and I'm black. [Shawna, 20, perceived as black]

Biracial individuals who appear white are well aware of the fact that people are treated differently according to the pigmentation of their skin.

I'm white skinned, so you know people don't treat me differently. The people who would treat someone differently because of their skin color don't treat me differently because I have white skin. [Sarah, 19, perceived as white]

Biracial persons who appear white are assumed to be white by the larger society. Therefore, they share many of the same advantages of those highest up in the racial hierarchy in the United States—white Americans.

Most remarkably, race need not be a priority for young biracial Americans who appear white. All but one of the biracial persons interviewed who maintain that race is not an important issue in their lives appear white. Jeanne, one interviewee who appears white, understands this.

I pass for white most of the time. Unless people start looking very carefully and then they're like "Huh?" That, I think, makes race less of an issue for me. [Jeanne, 18, perceived as white]

In the United States, it is only white persons, or those who appear white, who do not have to deal consistently with the issue of race throughout their lives. People view her as white, a member of the racial majority, so race does not have to be a major concern for Jeanne.

Appearing black also has consequences for racial self-definition. Both the interviewees under thirty and those over thirty who appear black tend to identify as black. Nine of the younger set of interviewees identify as black. Of those nine, eight have obvious African heritage. Five appear black, while three are perceived to be a mixture of both black and another race, and one looks Hispanic. Nine of the fourteen interviewees over thirty who appear predominantly black identify as black, while two define themselves as both black and biracial and the other three identify as biracial. Clearly, this evidence indicates that racial appearance is a key factor in determining racial self-identification among biracial persons.

The influence of racial appearance has limits, however. One of the most interesting aspects of the sixty-two interviews utilized in this research is that not one of the sixty-two mixed-race persons self-identified as white. Although sixteen of the sixty-two *appear* completely white, none identify as merely white. The transformation stops just short of a complete dismissal of the "one drop rule." While an increasing number of biracial persons feel free to identify as both black and white, none go so far as to ignore their African heritage.

My research indicates that the college-age U.S. population reflects the attitude of biracial Americans. Two hundred and four New England-area college students were asked to respond to the following question: *Should those who have both an African American and a white parent be racially defined as (A) white (B) black (C) biracial?*[3] The vast majority (74%) of the respondents believe that those with both a black and a white parent should be racially identified as biracial. However, while only 4 percent espouse the traditional "one drop rule," not one of the two hundred and four respondents believe that those with both an African American and a white parent should be defined as white.

It is still not socially acceptable for a biracial person who appears white to identify racially as white. They are, however, now able to define themselves as *both* black and white. This is a remarkable change from the dominant "one drop rule" ideology of the pre–Civil Rights era. The historical influences of the Civil Rights Movement and the repercussions of the Movement heavily influenced this transformation.

HISTORICAL INFLUENCES ON THE TRANSFORMATION

Anselm Strauss, working within a theory of identity, writes that "personal identity is meshed with group identity, which itself rests upon an historical past" [Strauss, 1959:173]. As noted previously, history critically influences both individual and group identity. Moreover, transformations in identity are often tied to particular changes from one epoch to another in history. In this most recent racial identity transformation of biracial individuals, the onset and influence of the Civil Rights era provided the major catalyst for the change.

It is widely acknowledged that the Civil Rights Movement had a major impact on black identity and interracial relations. What is not as well known is that this movement also played a major role in the transformation of racial identity among biracial individuals. With the advent of equality, the separation of the white and black races no longer found a basis in legislation. Under law it no longer mattered whether you were black or white. Legal equality among the races had been established. While prejudice still existed in U.S. society, with this legislation, the "one drop rule" no longer carried with it the threat of official second-class citizenship for all persons found to have any African ancestry.

On the heels of the Civil Rights Acts, the 1967 *Loving v. Virginia* decision cleared all legal barriers to interracial marriage. As described in Chapter 1, the invalidation of miscegenation legislation was a strong influence in the transformation of the racial identity of biracial Americans. Black/white interracial marriages increased in number after the *Loving* verdict. More important, however, these marriages prompted a "baby boom" of legitimate biracial children. "The number of children born to black/white couples has doubled since 1980" [Sándor, 6/94:38,39]. In turn, this demographic "boom" in mixed-race children has begun to challenge the existing monoracial racial structure. Today, it is no longer uncommon to have one or more children in a classroom who refuse to conform to directions that instruct them to label themselves as one race or as an "other."

Ironically, however, those biracial persons coming of age during the Civil Rights battles of the 1960s were much more likely to adopt the "one drop rule" than today's biracial young adults. In their cases, however, it would be the version of the "rule" that was adopted by the black nationalist movement. Instead of viewing black "blood" as a "drop" of shame, members of the black nationalist movement touted their African background. They appropriated it from the white "racists" and claimed it for themselves. At the same time, Movement politics made it clear that anyone who had an African ancestor should do the same. "After the 1960s, many Black leaders insisted that all people of any degree of Black heritage must identify themselves as Black and give up any identification with their White ancestry." Many biracial Americans who grew up at this time concurred [Spickard, 1989:338].

In further upending the traditional degradation of dark-skinned Americans, black Americans began to go through a "rite of passage" by adopting, in some cases, personal names that reflected African ancestry and by changing the name that referred to their race from Negro to black or Afro-American. According to Anselm Strauss [1959:16], there is an "indissoluble tie between name and self-image." Changing one's name indicates "a rite of passage" in which persons choose new names that they believe represent themselves more closely than the ones previously assigned to them. In the late sixties and early seventies, those of African descent began to scorn the word "Negro" and refer to themselves as either Afro-American or "black," a term from which many African Americans had historically tried to distance themselves.

Throughout history, the word "black" had always carried with it negative connotations. In the epoch of the Black power movement, though, blackness became something in which to take pride. "Black" had become "beautiful." Floyd McKissick, the black nationalist leader of CORE (Congress of Racial Equality) announced that "1966 shall be remembered as the year we left our imposed status as Negroes and became *Black Men*" [quoted in Sitkoff, 1981:215].

Biracial Americans of this era viewed their racial self-definition as black, or Afro-American, as a political statement. Instead of embracing a new name for themselves that emphasized both sides of their racial heritage, these mixed-race persons chose to strengthen and affirm the only part of their racial identity recognized by U.S. society. While the terms *black* and *Afro-American* still emphasized only the African part of their heritage, within the context of the Civil Rights Movement, black Americans changed the connotations of the words from negative to positive.

Within the larger social transformation, each individual must come to terms with and adopt a rationale around his or her own personal identity. "Most people, throughout most of history, have reflected the cultures they grew up in" [McCall and Simmons, 1966/1978:251]. During a period of societal transformation in group identity, many individuals go through their own personal changes in self-identity in concert with the larger society. The following examples show how various individuals do this.

Some black-white Americans who lived through the Civil Rights era and who recognize their biraciality note that their racial self-definition is also politically based. Chris, a thirty-seven-year-old who defines himself as both black and biracial, says his decision not to identify as white is politically based.

I'm sure you might be curious as to why I don't identify as being white. I think these definitions, if anything, are political. I believe for someone to be white they have certain privileges which I am not privy to. And therefore I don't identify with that. And it's a generational thing to some degree. Within this country, anyone who had any kind of drop of black blood was automatically assumed to be black. And we grew up with that understanding. [Chris, 37, perceived as black]

Chris's self-definition was influenced by the entangled forces of history and politics. Raised by parents who were heavily influenced by the "one drop rule," Chris took his decision not to identify as white one step further. For him, it is a personal decision based upon societal realities, while for his parents and others of the preceding generation, there was no *decision* needed for him to identify as black; it was simply reality. If you were biracial before the Civil Rights era, you *were* black in the eyes of U.S. society.

During the Civil Rights Movement, some biracial persons combined political activism with a strong desire to be accepted by the black community. Historically, biracial persons were more easily, though begrudgingly, accepted by the black than by the white community. The "one drop rule" prevented them from ever being a truly equal member of white society. For light-skinned biracial persons not readily accepted by either whites or blacks, the Civil Rights era became a time when they could "prove" their allegiance to black America. As activists, they could establish the truth of their blackness.

Zenobia Kujichagulia, a forty-three-year-old biracial woman who identifies as black, speaks of how her efforts as a black activist helped win her the loyalty of the black community. Growing up, she had been spurned by both the black and white communities at various times in her life. These rejections both hurt and angered Zenobia. It was her work with the Black Panthers, during the Civil Rights era, that enabled her to become a legitimate member of black activist society.

I started getting involved with the Black Panther Party. . . . I was able to really establish myself fully in the party with my beliefs and my experience and channel that rage and all of that hurt into constructive action and be accepted. That was very good. [Zenobia Kujichagulia, 43, perceived as white, mixed, or a light-skinned black][4]

On the other hand, there are those biracial people who grew up in the sixties and seventies who define themselves as black based on what they consider to be reality rather than on politics. These older biracial persons represent what Strauss refers to as "an old guard which maintains that the situation has not really changed at all" [1959:26]. These persons establish their racial self-definition on what they believe to be actuality rather than on politics or ideology. They adopt a structural perspective of their situation, maintaining that it is society, rather than individuals, that determines racial identity. They espouse the belief that biracial individuals will always be considered and treated as blacks in this society and those who try to identify themselves differently will be defeated in their attempt. These structuralists do not believe it is possible for individuals to change society. The majority of the interviewees who are over thirty fall into this category. According to these individuals, a biracial person who considers himself or herself anything but black is living in a fantasy land. For these people of mixed-race descent, their experience has taught them that being biracial is not an option in the United States. They believe the category simply does not exist.

Susan is a good example of biracial persons who do not believe it possible to be anything but black. As we saw in her case study, she grew up in a family known as the "Negro family" in her suburban California town. Acknowledging the prevailing racial structure of the day, Susan's family accepted and embraced their identification as black. Her experience being labeled and treated as black by both her family and the larger society has encouraged Susan's understanding that individuals must succumb to society's determination of racial identification. Her belief that "the theory of race as it's used in this culture does not allow for anything else" is shared by other biracial persons who have undergone similar experiences.

Another interviewee, Joe, born in the year the *Loving* verdict was overturned, shares Susan's point of view. While not quite thirty, he is old enough to have been influenced by the remnants of pre-Civil Rights era racial ideology. He declares that U.S. society makes a person of both black and white heritage an African American. He believes that every child of mixed racial descent has to come to terms with the fact that it is society, and not themselves, that determines how they should be defined racially. For many biracial persons, this is of major importance in their lives. They believe it is simply impossible to change the prevailing attitudes in society.

That's probably the greatest issue that biracial children have to deal with. It's not about how you perceive yourself. It's about how you are perceived. And the very fact of the matter is that in this society you are African American. [Joe, 28, perceived as black]

Moreover, says Joe, if the child is a little slow in firmly embracing his or her identity as a black person, but yet appears black or is known to have black heritage, society will give him or her a forceful push in that direction. He distinctly remembers his societal shove toward his identity as an African American.

If you're confused, the world lets you know very quickly. I can remember as a little boy going into the store which was right across the street from my house and having a guy who was Italian who was the manager of the store call me "nigger" in Italian. [Joe, 28, perceived as black]

Joe recalls that this incident helped make it very clear to him at an early age that society perceives him as black.

On the other hand, most of the parents of biracial children born after the Civil Rights Movement believe that it *is* possible to change society. The Civil Rights successes of the sixties heavily influenced many of the parents of the "biracial baby boomers." In keeping with the spirit of the Movement, a large number of these couples fiercely believe that race should no longer be an issue in our society. As

Herbert Mead pointed out, because human beings are able to think, they can displace traditional meanings and societal norms with new ways of doing and perceiving [Mead, 1934]. These parents are good examples of Mead's thoughts on the power of human agency. In their own lives, they refused to abide by the customary racial norms and, in large part due to the changing historical and cultural epoch, managed to stand fast and endure. Disgusted with the prevailing importance of race, they are determined to undermine the prevailing racial norms and create new ones. Having crossed racial boundaries themselves and survived, many view their children as symbols of an end to those barriers. In turn, they do not discuss race with their biracial children or, if they do, they emphasize to their offspring that they contain the "best of both worlds." These interracial parents do not acknowledge the white-initiated "one drop rule."

The majority of the interviewees who identify as biracial are the offspring of this type of parent. The parents in the case studies consisting of the under-thirty cohort barely spoke about race with their children. Cheryl, a twenty-year-old interviewee, revealed that the only time her and her sister Jeanne's parents spoke about their racial background was when they assured them they could write down "anything they wanted" when filling out forms with racial categories. Rasheed's only recollection of discussing race with his parents was when he asked his mother "what he was" and she calmly told him, "Your father is black and I'm German and English." "Race was never an issue for anyone" when he was growing up. Not surprisingly, Cheryl, Jeanne, and Rasheed all define themselves as both black and white.

Another under-thirty interviewee, Luke, is also the offspring of such parents. He describes how his father helped form his identity as a biracial person.

From the day I was a little kid, my father was always like, "You can't deny your mother, you can't deny me. You're both. You're mixed. And don't let anyone take that away from you." [Luke, 21, perceived as black or Hispanic]

Always keeping in mind the words of his father on the subject, Luke is determined to maintain his identify as both black and white.

Clearly the cohort of interviewees born after the Civil Rights Movement perceive of themselves racially in a manner different from those biracial persons over the age of thirty. Mixed-race persons who choose to call themselves biracial, or both black and white, are going through "a rite of passage" similar to what Strauss describes. They have rebelled against the traditional use of the word "black" to describe themselves and have chosen, instead, a title they believe portrays both aspects of their racial identity.

INFLUENCE OF CULTURE

U.S. culture has also prompted the transformation of racial identity. The children who comprise the "biracial baby boom" have had more than laws and racial appearance influence their racial self-definition. As discussed in Chapter 1, the major liberalization and individualization that developed in the sixties and seventies tremendously influenced the transformation. These cultural shifts sparked group identity politics in which many biracial Americans are now immersed.

The multicultural movement, which began in the seventies, also had a huge effect on "biracial baby boomers," as they did on the rest of America. These young adults were the first generation to be taught that diversity is good. Multiculturalism was popular during the majority of their lives. Being unique began to be viewed as a positive rather than a negative trait by society. Noncomformity was admired. Racial and ethnic distinctions were no longer relegated to food and holidays. As people sought out and began to embrace their various racial and ethnic roots, it was only natural for many biracial Americans to identify with both sides of their racial heritage. As the American culture embraced multiculturalism, support groups for interracial couples and their offspring were formed.[5] For the first time in American history, black/white couples received support from society. Increasing social acceptance enabled biracial persons to proclaim both sides of their racial background.

Some biracial individuals who themselves identify as black have noticed the transformation. Society, according to some, has become less rigidly divided racially. Joe, whose racial identity was firmly cemented by the reactions of those with whom he interacted, acknowledges that the racial atmosphere is somewhat different now.

Interview anyone in college now who is biracial. They were probably born in a time when we were more tolerant. In 1967, when I was born, we weren't. To be born in '76, '77, I think we're tolerant as a society. We were strictly defined in the sixties, black and white. . . . You stood out. Black and white don't stand out that much anymore. Not as much as they used to. [Joe, 28, perceived as black]

Other mixed-race interviewees who identify as black have also noted the transformation. Barbara, a forty-eight-year-old interviewee, believes that young biracial persons today racially define themselves very differently from black-white Americans of her own generation. She maintains that "there is now this whole recognition that mixed-race people can be a separate entity. They can be whomever they want to be." There are also simply more biracial persons now than there were when Barbara was a child.

The increasing number of biracial persons has certainly influenced the ongoing transformation of racial identity. The old adage "strength in numbers" rings true here. As Strauss notes, when "certain alienated persons eventually discover that others are facing similar problems and experiences . . . new terminologies arising out of these discoveries are shared products" [Strauss, 1959:38]. It makes sense that mixed-race persons may first feel at ease defining themselves as biracial when they meet another person who defines him/herself in that manner. Much like members of other interest groups, biracial Americans are beginning to recognize that they share a similar struggle with thousands of other Americans. The rise in interracial marriages and biracial births has brought with it a whole new terminology to describe black-white Americans racially. No longer are biracial persons so small in numbers that, in order to survive racially, they must somehow try to blend into already existing racial structures and definitions.

One interviewee's own racial identity development is a microcosm of the societal transformation. Twenty-year-old Jason's story echoes the societal transformation process that began during the Civil Rights Movement. This larger transformation began when biracial persons became immersed in the social changes evolving with the inception of the Civil Rights era. Being black became a source of pride. The multicultural movement, emerging from the Civil Rights era and identity politics, encouraged many biracial persons to realize that, while being black is good, acknowledging their white, as well as their black heritage, gives them a fuller sense of self. Gaining strength in numbers through the "biracial baby boom" and in spirit and social support through the multicultural movement, biracial Americans began to embrace both sides of their racial identity.

In a parallel fashion, Jason went through his own process of racial identity transformation. Unlike most parents of the "biracial baby boom" cohort, Jason's mother and father raised their son to believe in the "one drop rule." They taught him that he was black. Like Susan and her parents, they believed that "our culture [will] not allow for anything else." Jason, however, raised during the multicultural movement and eager to acknowledge both sides of his racial heritage, embarked upon his own "rite of passage" and declared himself to be both black and white. This "passage" began in junior high when he began to read such seminal works on the history of African Americans as Lerone Bennett's *Before the Mayflower* [1987]. Books such as Bennett's sparked Jason to delve into his own racial background. In doing so, he became interested in both his black and white ancestors. He describes his racial identity transformation from black to biracial as a decision to stop "denying" half of his racial background.

Basically throughout my life, my parents have told me that I'm black. And, I think, probably when I was a junior in high school, I realized that it was unhealthy for me to just say that I was black. Plus, I thought it was denying part of myself.

Why do you think your parents kept telling you that you were black?

Probably because they're part of society. Society was going to look at me as being black. And at that time I think that they felt like they needed to brace me for that. [Jason, 20, perceived as black]

Despite his parents's definition and society's perception of his being black, Jason has declared that he is both black and white. Of course, it is possible that even if he had been born thirty years earlier, his racial identity would be the same. It is clear, however, that society, while not necessarily encouraging, is much more accepting of his choice to embrace both sides of his racial identity today than it was a mere few decades ago. U.S. culture has increasingly become both diverse and accepting of diversity. If he wants to, Jason can now turn to multiracial groups for support. He can seek out—and find—college students his age who are also biracial. If his biraciality is challenged, Jason can say he is simply following the example of such popular figures as Mariah Carey or Chelsi Smith, Miss USA 1995, who made "her experience as a biracial woman" a hallmark of her reign as Miss USA [Winchester, 4/95–5/95:36].

If Jason fails to sway his challengers, he can find inspiration in golfing phenomenon Tiger Woods, arguably the most popular and hippest mixed-race young American today. Woods has fought back against the media's attempts to define him racially as black. He firmly declares himself to be "Cablinasian," a term he created as a child to ensure complete representation of his Caucasian, black, Asian, and American Indian background [Leland, 5/5/97:59].

Numerous aspects of U.S. culture that did not exist thirty years ago support Jason's declaration of being both black and white, including increasing social acceptance of interracial couples and their offspring, larger numbers of biracial persons, multiculturalism, and the continual creation of group identity movements. While many new segments of U.S. culture encourage the transformation of biracial identity, for the individual, their influence takes effect in his or her immediate social setting.

INFLUENCE OF IMMEDIATE SOCIAL SETTING

One of the most telling signs of a transformation in racial identity among biracial individuals is that there is now no longer a singular way to define them racially. While the traditional racial structure and many of its operating tools, such as racial categories on forms from the SATs to the Census, maintain the "one drop rule," the survey described at the beginning of this chapter indicates that most young Americans are now in favor of multiracial categories. It is clear, however, that one's immediate environment, as well as racial appearance, historical period, and prevailing culture, plays a role in the individual racial identification of biracial persons. Indeed, it is in one's particular social setting that the influence of racial appearance, historical period, and prevailing culture plays itself out. Individuals are directly affected by these societal influences through their family, peers, and economic environment. When in an ambiguous situation, humans tend to conform to the majority opinion [Asch, 1952]. If a biracial person feels any uncertainty about his or her racial identity, the person will undoubtedly look to the immediate environment for cues. Valerie, a biracial college student, understands this.

If you were to put a whole bunch of us together, you would find so many different attitudes and so many different mentalities. I think a lot of it is economics, who you were raised by, what your surroundings [are], and what company you keep. I think those are four factors in determining an identity. [Valerie, 18, perceived as black]

The racial self-definition of biracial individuals is, at least in part, a function of economic class. The poorer the biracial individual, the greater the chance he or she will live in a neighborhood with a high percentage of African Americans. Living among predominantly African Americans will, in turn, increase the likelihood that the biracial person will identify racially as black. Six of the nine interviewees under the age of thirty who identify as black were raised in either a diverse or predominantly black neighborhood. Four of those nine came from families they described as barely, or lower than, middle class.

Five of the nine biracial individuals under thirty who came from poorer backgrounds identify more with the black community than the white community. In many instances, it appears as if a sense of pride in being black was used as a substitute for material wealth. The connection between racial identity and class may also be due to the fact that racial identity is increasingly static at lower economic levels due to financial constraints resulting in decreased mobility and freedom to escape boundaries. Valerie aptly explains the connection between race and class for many.

When I was more in the upper and middle class, those were the times that my [black] father would tell me I'm a prima donna and I would act like a "white girl." Whereas being in a poorer environment now, and being at the bottom again, it's like I can really identify a lot more with the black race. I'm not in that uppity kind of mentality. [Valerie, 18, perceived as black]

Valerie's racial identity fluctuated with her economic status. Accused by her father of acting like a "white girl" when financially comfortable, Valerie, now poor, strongly identifies with the black community. For Valerie, being black and being poor are directly related.

Peer relations are also very important in the racial self-definition process of a biracial person. Friends are highly influential in the socialization process. They affect the goals of the individual: what one strives for and whom one wants to become. Friends often also inform people about who they are. When evaluating one's identity, the reactions of others must be taken into account [McCall and Simmons, 1966/1978]. Brandon, who identifies as black, describes the influence of the children he interacted with as a boy on his racial self-determination.

When I was younger, I used to look in the mirror and say, "What am I?" And I was confused a little bit. But I think the point at which I started defining myself as black was when the black community started regarding me as being black. If you're black, there are certain things that are said to one another that somebody who is white wouldn't say. And they started showing me they accepted me by saying those things when I was in high school and late in junior high, and they just kept doing it, and nobody ever labeled me as being white when I was in school. [Brandon, 24, perceived as black]

As Strauss states, "it is obvious in self-appraisal [that] the responses of others must be taken into account" [1959:34]. Interactionist theorists note that we derive our sense of self through interacting with others. We see ourselves as we imagine others see us [Cooley, 1902]. Being treated as black by his black classmates and as nonwhite by his white classmates clearly influenced Brandon's decision to identify as black rather than as biracial.

Most biracial young persons today, however, do not have experiences similar to Brandon's. The majority grow up surrounded by predominantly white children. Throughout the twentieth century, "class homogamy has prevailed" in most interracial marriages. Most black/white marriages have taken place among the middle and professional classes [Spickard, 1989].[6] Because most of those who marry interracially are well situated economically, many young biracial adults have been raised in either an integrated neighborhood or, more likely, a predominantly white area. In turn, this has led to many biracial people "never [having] had any black friends cause there weren't any around" [Beth, 20, perceived as white].

Even in the high schools, little interaction between biracial and black students takes place. Although there has been an effort to maximize diversity of schools through busing, many schools still reflect the racial compositions of the neighborhoods in which they are located. Many interviewees attended high school with few, if any, African Americans.

In my high school, there was maybe like three or four Asian people and then my sister and I and then there was like one other black kid. That's it. So most of my friends were white when I was growing up. [Beth, 20, perceived as white]

In many instances, even in schools in which there are large numbers of African American students, tracking[7] separates black and biracial students.

I was in honors and the Advanced Placement track, so until I took a college prep class in my senior year, there was not a single black student in any of my classes. So that also made it difficult to know any of them because I never saw any of them. [Yolanda, 18, perceived as black]

Economic class, friends, and classmates notwithstanding, the family tends to be the most important factor in a person's life. It follows that how the parents of biracial individuals racially define their offspring will play a major role in how biracial persons will identify themselves throughout their lives. Black/white couples who grew up before the Civil Rights era would most likely identify their children as black. That was the clear choice to make at the time. The law, culture, and often their children's racial appearance and immediate social environment defined their offspring as black. In order to prepare their progeny to face and understand how they would be treated in society, these parents chose a strategy that made it clear to their sons and daughters that they were black. For instance, Chris's and Susan's parents told them, directly, that they were black in a straightforward attempt to brace them for the way they would be perceived by society.

Today, however, reflecting the culture of the time, many parents of biracial children raise them to embrace both sides of their racial heritage. Other interracial couples treat race as a nonissue in their households. Cheryl's parents, and Rasheed's parents are typical of this second type. As seen earlier, they volunteered little information to their children concerning their race, merely saying that however they chose to define themselves was acceptable. These types of parents have taken it upon themselves and their children to challenge and alter the prevailing racial structure. The fact that only nine of the thirty-two interviewees under the age of thirty identify as black is evidence of this trend.

Of course, these families are *able* to affect the present racial structure because of what has happened in the larger social settings of law and culture. Because of the societal changes that have occurred since the Civil Rights era, there are now more opportunities for individual choice in racial self-definitions. In turn, these individual decisions contribute to the ongoing societal transformation of racial identity among biracial individuals.

NO MORE RACIAL CLASSIFICATIONS?

Classifications are inherently value laden. They "not only carry our anticipations but also those values that were experienced when we encountered the . . . persons . . . now classified" [Strauss, 1959:23]. Traditionally, in the white-dominated racial structure found in the United States, blacks have been treated with the greatest disdain of any racial group. Moreover, racial definitions are compounded by class definitions. The fact that a large number of black Americans live in the lower classes[8] creates the illusion that one's social class is somehow derived directly from one's race. The Social Darwinistic premise that black Americans maintain a "culture of poverty"[9] that perpetuates their existence in the lower classes is given legitimacy by this unfounded leap from race/culture to economic class.

Therefore, being identified as either black or white carries with it great social connotations. Your life chances are immediately altered based upon your racial classification. As Susan states, young biracial persons

understand that there are power and privilege issues connected to whom they choose to be. And the culture says if you're black you are connected somehow to welfare, and you're connected somehow with crime, and you're connected somehow with all these bad things, not with the economic survival of America, which is the truth. [Susan, 46, perceived as white]

Aside from the negative repercussions, classifications serve a very useful purpose in society. They help persons make order out of chaos. "The act of identifying objects, human or physical, allows a person to organize his action with reference to those objects. . . . You must identify social situations in order to cope with them" [Strauss, 1959:45]. The present racial classification system in the United States is becoming increasingly problematic, however. Mixed-race persons do not fit into the existing categories. As a result, people are often misguided in their attempts to identify racially a biracial person.

For instance, when Cheryl was a baby, strangers who peered at her explained

her dark skin by assuming her white mother must have left her out in the sun, exclaiming, "You're baby has such a beautiful tan!" Cheryl understands how important people feel it is to be able to classify persons whom they encounter. It is so critical for some that they will attempt, as she puts it, "to make sense of things in a way that doesn't make sense" if it will give them the peace of mind of fitting someone into a preexisting category.

Today, however, alongside the transformation of racial identity among biracial persons, there is a growing rebellion against all racial classifications. The survey described earlier in this chapter indicates such a trend. Of those questioned, 8.8 percent refused to answer based on their belief that people should be able to choose their own racial self-definition. Another 6.3 percent of those surveyed volunteered their opinion that we should do away with "labeling" people. Clearly, some people are beginning to perceive racial classifications as arbitrary, confining, and simply wrong. When imagining a world without racial labels, they envision freedom rather than chaos.

For people of mixed-race descent, racial classifications can be especially disconcerting. However, all have grown up filling out forms that provided no biracial or mixed racial option. Many of the younger interviewees volunteered their resentment of having had to define themselves on these monoracially focused forms. Cory, a college student, is one such frustrated individual. When asked what she would label herself if she had to identify herself racially, she responded as a participant in the rebellion against all racial designations.

I wouldn't. I've been unidentifying myself for a very long time, and I wouldn't start now. [Stacy, 18, perceived as black]

Throughout her life, Stacy has fought off any and all racial labels. She has consistently refused to complete racial classification forms. During her childhood, this resulted in numerous confrontations with irritated teachers. While it has been a lonely quest for her, she is not alone in her struggle.

CONCLUSION

Multiracial people have demanded new classifications for several years.[10] Americans who want to throw out racial designations in general have now joined the fray. They do not believe society will founder in confusion and turmoil if its traditional racial structure collapses. Whether or not they are correct in their assessment of the importance of racial classifications is debatable. What is clear, however, is that the racial structure is being challenged as never before.

Community and class now have gained more influence over the construction of race than skin color. Biracial Americans, like black Americans, are becoming increasingly stratified between those who have money and those who do not. Black-white persons who are members of poor communities are much more likely to identify as simply black than are those who are at least middle class. While

Susan states that, in our society, blackness is associated with crime and degradation, there is, however, a growing sense among Americans of two types of black persons: those who are economically comfortable and can blend in with middle- and upper-class white America and those who are poor, live in the inner city, and are to be avoided. While the former are now, for the most part, accepted into white professional society, the latter's blackness is imprinted on them as a mark of inferiority. In the eyes of much of white America, the economic situation and the race of lower-class blacks are integrally connected. They are poor because they are black. Today biracial Americans are black if they are poor and are biracial if they are in the middle or upper class.

Most biracial Americans who are financially well situated have few black Americans as role models. They live in predominantly white neighborhoods and attend majority white schools. Indeed, their one parent who is black implicitly promotes interacting with white persons. They seem to have little, if anything, in common with poor black Americans. It is no wonder young biracial persons recognize their white heritage. The true question is why more do not consider themselves exclusively white. The fact that they cannot be white reveals that while the "significance of race" may have "declined" [Wilson, 1987], it has not entirely dissipated. The "one drop rule," while defeated, still exerts some power.

The concept of race, instead of fading, is shifting. The transformation in racial identity of biracial persons is a prominent example of the transmutation of race in this nation. While it is increasingly acceptable for black-white persons to claim both their black and their white heritage, the possibility of their being simply white is still not socially sanctioned. The boundaries between black and white have moved, but they still exist.

As traditional racial demarcations change, so do social interactions between biracial and monoracial persons. As young, black-white Americans recognize both their racial heritages, they cross historic racial boundaries in all aspects of their life—personal and public. No area in the private lives of biracial persons is more scrutinized than their romantic experiences. Biracial men and women must confront the fact that many persons perceive whom they date as a determination of how they identify racially. The reactions they receive in the dating world make it painfully clear that race still divides U.S. society. For the majority of young biracial men and women, dating is a "turning point" in their racial identity. Chapter 4 examines the dating experiences of biracial college students.

NOTES

1. I had originally hypothesized that the biracial person would tend to identify racially with the same sex parent. Upon examination of the data, however, I found there to be no such correlation (or any other correlation between the sex and race of the parent and the racial identity of the adult child).

2. Racial appearance is defined by the interviewee in describing how he/she believes a typical American stranger would define him/her racially.

3. The results of the survey are as follows: 74.0% said biracial, 4.4% said black, 8.8% refused to answer saying the person should choose for him/her self, 6.3% refused to answer on the basis that we should not label people, .09% refused to answer saying it depends on the appearance of the individual, and 5.3% refused to answer without comment.

4. Transcript found in Funderburg, 1994.

5. Such groups as "A Place for Us" in Gardena, California, the "Biracial Family Network" in Chicago, the "Biracial Family Resource Center" in New York, and the "Interracial Family Alliance" in Philadelphia are relatively common now throughout the United States [Spickard, 1989:376; The Oprah Winfrey Show, 1995].

6. From personal observation, I cannot help but think that this is changing. I see more and more young lower- and working-class black/white couples.

7. A system of "ranking" students according to academic ability. For reasons from outright discrimination by teachers to institutional discrimination due to race-biased tests, a disproportionate number of students assigned to the lower-level ranks are lower-class and minority students.

8. The median household income for whites is $27,427, while the median income for African American families is $15,475. One in ten white Americans live in poverty while one in three African Americans live below the poverty level [Horton and Smith, 1994:405].

9. For a discussion of the "culture of poverty" theory, see Steinberg, 1989:106–127.

10. A rally in Washington, D.C. of mixed-race persons demanding a change in the Census 2000 form took place on July 20, 1996.

4
Turning Points: Biracial College Students and Dating

One arena in which the struggle over biracial racial identity is most intense is dating. More than simply an outward sign of hormonal growth, the onset of dating for biracial Americans is a critical juncture in the public and private racial lives of these young people. Upon entering the dating world, many biracial men and women directly confront, for the first time, the fact that they are "different." In our monoracial society, biracial individuals face intense pressure to identify with one race. Choosing which race to date is one means of establishing a racial self-identity. Dating has therefore become a racial tug-of-war in which biracial persons are the rope. Biracial Americans feel they must choose sides—white or black. More than merely selecting a romantic partner, the biracial person is seen as embracing a race.

Outward signs of a biracial person embracing his or her white heritage are met with various forms of condemnation from both the white and black populations. Dating a white person is viewed as one such sign. As seen below, a biracial individual who dates white people must confront disapproval from all sides. The dating world is a major racial battleground that biracial Americans must traverse.

Battle lines typically form where there is a relatively small population of African Americans. Black/white interracial marriage in the United States is most predominant in areas in which relatively few black Americans reside. All forms of interracial relationships are most apt to take place when there is only a small number of racial minorities in the midst of a large number of the racial majority. For black/white marriages in particular, "there is a strong inverse relationship between relative group size and outmarriage: the smaller the proportion of blacks in a state, the greater the percentage of blacks who marry whites" [Kalmijm, 1993]. It follows, therefore, that the biracial offspring of these marriages will grow up in predominantly white neighborhoods.

The majority of the interracial couples in these neighborhoods consist of a black man and a white woman. According to the 1985 U.S. Census, there are approximately three times more black males who are married to nonblacks than there are black females who marry outside their race. As black women gain in economic status and the pool of eligible black males declines, the gap is beginning to narrow. Because most married interracial couples are in the middle or professional classes, the majority of black-white biracial children of married couples most likely grow up in neighborhoods that are at least middle class economically.

While many biracial Americans grow up in economically comfortable surroundings similar to the middle-class ideal, many of their experiences are atypical of the average middle-class young person. Unlike most children, biracial girls and boys do not necessarily racially resemble either of their biological parents. In many ways, they have to forge their own racial path in our society. For instance, they cannot simply follow the racial dating and mating pattern of their parents.

The dating and mating choices of biracial Americans are unique in our society. Children of both a black and a white individual, biracial men and women are literally unable to follow in their parents' footsteps. Moreover, for many biracial Americans, dating is an experience rife with the varied racial opinions of their social network. Instead of being a private relationship between two people, it becomes a public discussion of racial alliance or rejection.

This chapter focuses on the dating experiences of biracial college students. In doing so, it examines two critical "turning points" in the lives of biracial Americans: dating and college life. For many, their early experiences with dating opened their eyes to the fact that they are different from their monoracial peers. Many were surprised and dismayed to find that parents of longtime friends did not approve of their dating their son or daughter. Their African heritage was no longer acceptable when friendship turned to romance. When biracial Americans attend college,[1] dating becomes even more complicated. Suddenly they are forced to "choose sides"—white or black. In many cases, their dating life becomes the "litmus test" that determines which side they have "chosen."

CHOOSING SIDES

On racially polarized college campuses across America, biracial students struggle to find a place for themselves. For many, it is difficult, if not impossible, to straddle both the white and the black communities on campus. In most instances, the minority black student body demands full allegiance. In their eyes, a biracial person, especially one who appears black, should identify first and foremost with the African American community. In turn, their friends and their dates should come from the black student body.

To be accepted as a member of the African American community on campus, biracial students must act "black." In some cases, this means they must embrace a culture different from that in which they were raised. A freshman spoke of the pressure she feels to be "down" if she wants to be accepted by the African

American community on campus.

Oh I'm not. I'm not ghetto. I mean. . . . It's awful. Because there are all these stereotypes of what the black experience is, you know. It's like you listen to rap, you're from the ghetto, you wear baggy clothes, you talk hard. I don't do that. I mean, I do listen to rap. I do wear some of that, but I don't take on that whole persona because it's not my background.

Would you want to?

No, not particularly. I like the friends I have and I think in order to be "down" I'd have to get rid of my white and Asian friends.

And why is that, do you think?

Because being "down" means keeping it black. Staying black. You know, black pride, all this stuff. And so for me I'd have to prove that I was "down," I think. I mean I don't know. Maybe these are all my stereotypes but that's what it seems. And I don't want to do that. I don't want to have to choose. And so by not choosing, the choice is made for me. Because I haven't made an effort to stay black, so I'm not. [Yolanda, freshman, perceived as black]

One means of "choosing" to be black is to join an African American campus organization. To a large extent, this also determines whom biracial students' friends will be and whom they will date. Just as most people meet dates through friends, so do biracial college students. If they are an active member of the African American group on campus, it is very likely they will meet both friends and romantic partners through the organization. This is particularly true if the black group on campus stresses the need for African American students to socialize exclusively among themselves. Many of those interviewed discussed how the African American groups on campus have made them feel obliged to choose between being white and being black.

I originally was involved in the African American group here on campus, and I went with them on trips and stuff. But it was, it came to the point where if I had other friends, you know, they didn't speak to me or they didn't say "hi." And so I just didn't like it, you know, that I either had to choose to be friends with them all the time or friends with you know the rest of the school, but forget about them. It's so, I don't know. I've really been trying to deal with that. It's, I don't like it. I don't like that situation at all. [Julia, freshman, perceived as black]

Among the biracial college students interviewed, there is a clear correlation between activism in race-related campus groups and whom biracial individuals date. Those who are active in a group such as the Black Student Union are much more likely to date African Americans than those who are not. By the same token, those who are active in interracial campus groups have a greater chance of dating a racially diverse group of people. However, only a small minority of college campuses have interracial groups.

Table 4.1
Whom the College Student Interviewees Date

	Primarily Blacks and Other Nonwhites	Primarily Whites	Multiple Races*	
Males	3	3	2	(n = 8)
Females**	2	5	6	(n = 13)

*This includes persons of both minority and white racial backgrounds.
**Three interviewees have not dated.

Table 4.2
Whom the College Student Interviewees Date According to Involvement in Race-Based Campus Groups

Males (n = 8)

	Primarily Blacks and Other Nonwhites	Primarily Whites	Multiple Races
Active in Black Group	1	0	0
Active in Interracial Group	1	0	0
Not Active	1	3	2

Females (n = 16)

	Primarily Blacks and Other Nonwhites	Primarily Whites	Multiple Races	Have Not Dated
Active in Black Group	2	0	3*	0
Active in Interracial Group	0	1	2**	0
Not Active	0	4	1	3

*These interviewees are only somewhat active.
**This includes one interviewee who dates white and mixed-race persons.

Few interracial groups exist on most college campuses. This has left biracial students seeking to identify with both sides of their racial heritage in a serious predicament. They must choose between being "black" and joining the African American group or not being a member and becoming at least somewhat estranged from the black community on campus. All this is quite a shock for the many biracial persons who have come from predominantly white neighborhoods.

DISCOVERY OF DIFFERENCE

For many biracial individuals, it is not until they enter the world of dating that they realize they do not completely fit into their homogeneous surroundings. The entrance into the "dating" world can begin as early as the prepubescent years when girls and boys begin to recognize each other as potential romantic partners. This freshman describes her foray into the dating world as a biracial individual in a wealthy white neighborhood this way:

Well, because of our financial situation [which she described as middle to upper middle class] it kind of situates you. Like all my friends were white. They just were. I mean that's who I was exposed to, that's who lived with me in the neighborhood. I don't even think I started to realize I was even different from anyone else until I was probably nine years old, eight or nine.

What happened when you were eight or nine that suddenly made you realize?

Boys. Boys happened when I was eight or nine. Boys made eight or nine very difficult for me. [Stacy, freshman, perceived as black]

This young woman recounted a sorry tale of being tormented by two young boys whose "romantic" overtures she had spurned. Each passed her a note in class asking her to "go out" with him. She sent both notes back with a "no" response. One boy was African American and the other was white. Both channeled their hurt feelings into a display of racial epithets they hurled Stacy's way. The black boy shouted at her that she was "contaminated" with white blood, while the white boy growled that she was "contaminated" with black blood. Even more unfortunate for Stacy is the fact that the nickname "contaminated" stuck with her for many tortured years.

Typical of many of those interviewed, Stacy found dating frustrating. The white boys with whom she attended her high school classes did not want to date her because she had a black parent. On the other hand, she had little in common with the black boys who were very attracted to her "good" hair and light skin and clamored to ask her out. The first whiffs of schoolyard crushes had brought home to her the fact that she was different from both her white and her black classmates.

Yolanda, a freshman, believes that being biracial at her particular high school contributed to her never having had a date.

I haven't really dated at all because, I mean, I guess, I don't know if I can blame it entirely on my skin, but there were no interracial couples at my high school. And since I wasn't down with the black kids, that only left me with the white kids, and none of them ever thought that I'd ever be interested in any of them or whatever or none of them were interested in me cause I was black. So I never really, I never dated in high school. [Yolanda, freshman, perceived as black]

In this instance, being biracial, but being socially and culturally similar to her white peers left this high school girl with no dating options. Like so many other young biracial men and women, she had made the discovery of her difference. When it came to dating, her white upper-middle-class culture separated her from those with a similar phenotype, and her race kept her apart from those with whom she was raised.

Even biracial individuals who have an active dating life have to face the fact that they do not fit neatly into white middle-class society.

It hadn't really become clear to me that I was that much different from anybody else until the summer before my senior year when I looked back on my high school dating experiences. I was sitting down and actually realized that I never dated a girl whose parents actually approved. [Steve, junior, perceived as black]

Steve had dated many girls when he was in high school. Without fail, though, their predominantly white upper-middle-class parents did not approve. Steve grew up in the same overwhelmingly white neighborhood as these girls. He is courteous to parents, both athletic and a good student, and accepted by one of the most prestigious colleges in the country. Steve is everything the parents of the girls he dated could want except one thing—he is biracial. It was not until he started dating that this racial distinction became completely clear to Steve. For Steve and for others, this is just one of the hardships that comes from stepping into the dating world.

HARDSHIPS OF BIRACIAL INDIVIDUALS AND DATING

Some of the hardships biracial individuals may encounter on the romantic scene are similar to those confronted by individuals who have two black parents. Depending upon their appearance and their openness about their racial background, they are likely targets for the racial discrimination that confronts African Americans today. Many Americans, of all races, still believe in the "one drop rule." Hence many biracial individuals are viewed and treated, by both black and white persons, as African Americans.

Another problem that may confront biracial Americans is that many are viewed through the lenses of stereotypes. For instance, the racial myth that all black-white women are "passionate" and "exotic" may encourage white men to believe they are desirable merely for sex, rather than for any long-term, committed relationship. On the other hand, many biracial women state that they are perceived by black men as merely light-skinned "trophies" and status symbols. Biracial men are also often the victims of racial myths. Those who appear and/or are perceived to be black are also subject to the stereotype that in romantic relationships black men are to be valued for their sexual prowess and little else. Those with light skin are taunted by their friends that women will date them merely for the color of their skin and the prestige that accompanies being "almost white."

It is also important to note that biracial Americans are far from immune to the pervasive power of these types of stereotypes. Many biracial people are believers, at least on some level, of these racial myths. These stereotypes affect both who is willing to date black-white Americans and whom many biracial individuals choose to date.

I always have problems with black guys because black guys are always . . . I don't know why it is, but black guys always look to light-colored black women and multiracial women for sex and stuff. And so the only times I hang out with black guys are when we're doing homework or something together. [Claire, junior, perceived as white]

Claire maintains that African American men believe the myth that light-colored women and multiracial women are attractive merely as sex objects. Her understanding of how black men view her has encouraged her to avoid dating them. Claire has also been bombarded with her mother's stereotypical opinion of African American males.

Well, my mother never lets me go out with black guys. She thinks that they're all like serial rapists and drug dealers and stuff. [Claire, junior, perceived as white]

Overall, like many other Americans, Claire has based her opinion of African American males on media-encouraged stereotypes.

There are hardships, however, that are unique to biracial individuals. They may experience a sense of isolation, feeling "not quite black enough" when around black people and "not quite white enough" when around white individuals. In turn, both blacks and whites may encourage this sense of isolation by either declaring outright or implying that biracial people are *not* white or black enough. This can encourage a sense of isolation and marginality among biracial individuals.[2]

Moreover, light-skinned biracial individuals face envy and resentment from some darker-skinned African Americans and mixed-race people. Brandon, a young man who dates only minorities, describes some typical commentary his predominantly black and biracial friends have made concerning his dating life.

The only time I've had a problem dating minorities is maybe from a friend or something like that who says, "the girl's with you because of the fact that you're light skinned, you're mixed." And they say a lot that the girls who would date me feel that they are better people . . . that they are looked upon in a better way because they're dating someone who is much lighter. And that is what society views as being the end all and be all. [Brandon, 24, perceived as black]

Brandon, who has avoided dating white women for fear of race-based difficulties, still has to confront judgments about his dating life that are centered around his race. As someone who appears to be a light-skinned black person, he has to deal with the color prejudices within the black community. Many darker-skinned African Americans perceive Brandon's popularity with black women to be merely the result of his skin tone. Many, too, envy both his attractiveness to women and the skin color they deem responsible for his appeal. In many instances, this envy can turn into resentment, fostering negative feelings toward Brandon and other biracial individuals with light skin. For Brandon, and for so many other biracial Americans, dating will always have its racial complications.

When it comes to dating, many monoracial people view the biracial person's choice of a "significant other" as something of a racial litmus test. Biracial individuals have to deal with the fact that many people will perceive the color of their date, or mate, as a declaration of their racial preference, or even their racial self-definition. This may promote disappointment or even hostility from monoracial people who believe the biracial person has made the wrong racial choice.

CONFRONTING THE RACIAL LITMUS TEST

After facing the fact that they are not monoracial like most of the teenagers around them, biracial individuals are confronted with a choice. Whom should they date? For some, the decision is made for them. For biracial persons with dark skin, it may be too difficult to date white people. If they are female, white males may not ask them out. If they are male, they may decide not to deal with the disapproval of parents of potential white dates. Those who do venture to date are faced with the racial litmus test. Many monoracial people view a biracial person's dating choices as a sign of which racial group they choose to identify as their own. Sometimes biracial people themselves may also look upon their date/mate choice in this way.

Some biracial individuals are eager to date a black person in order to fulfill the black "half" of themselves. Surrounded by white people, some fear they will lose any sense of their own blackness. This is particularly prevalent among the biracial women interviewees who appear white.

I don't think race would play a role in whom I eventually decide to be with. I used to, when I was younger, think that I'm probably going to marry a black man . . . maybe just to prove myself. I don't know why. To prove that I'm half black or something. I don't know. [Beth, junior, perceived as white]

While this young woman says she is now beyond the stage of feeling she has to date a black man to prove herself, this is a theme that runs through the discussions of many of the college students interviewed. For most, there is a struggle to reconcile their biracial background with a monoracial society. Dating is one area in which this friction is most pronounced.

Biracial Americans who appear white are often judged by different standards than darker mixed-race individuals when they face the racial litmus test. Those who appear white are assumed to be white by those in the larger society who are unaware of their heritage. Therefore, they share many of the same advantages of those highest up in the racial hierarchy in the United States—white Americans.

It is easier for those who look white to date white people—if they care to do so—for a number of reasons. Their European features are closer to the American,

Eurocentric stereotype of what is beautiful. Many of those interviewed who are perceived as white believe that because they look more white than black, many white people view them as more familiar and thus more "approachable" than African Americans or biracial individuals who appear to be black. Many biracial people who appear white are also able to avoid the label of "sellout" from the African American community. They are less frequently harassed by blacks than those who appear black if they choose to date white people.

Would you say that a person who is half black and half white who marries a white person, would you maybe question that person, think that "Oh, they're trying to be white?"

I don't really know because I've never seen it. I guess in a way, to be honest, it would depend on how they look. If they looked more white, or if they looked more black. Cause, I mean, I think that that's what did have a lot to do with shaping me.

So would you be more accepting of a biracial person who's lighter marrying a white person, than a biracial person who's darker marrying a white person?

Probably, yes. [Valerie, freshman, perceived as black]

Overall, however, a biracial person dating white people is usually frowned upon by the African American community on college campuses. More often than not, the biracial man or woman is expected to date only black persons.

Would they [the black community on campus] care if you dated a white person?

First of all, it's talked about a lot. And there's no real answer to it and it's a very emotional topic. There is a tension there. There's people who I know are black who date white. Other white students and some other black students don't like it. And you know who they are, because you can just feel it. You know, you can feel the tension. The way I look at it is, if someone doesn't want to be friendly with me because I am dating someone who is white, forget 'em, you know. In a way, they are kind of offending me. Because, you know, I'm dating somebody who is also a part of my race, so, whatever. It doesn't really bother me. [Luke, junior, perceived as black or Hispanic]

Luke shares the same attitude as many biracial males concerning interracial and biracial/white dating. Most biracial men are quite accepting of it.[3] They are, however, very aware that there are those who strongly oppose such romantic relationships. The males interviewed believe that black women have the hardest time dealing with biracial men dating white women.

Like black girls, especially, didn't like it that I'd go out with a white girl. And, I mean, I just thought that if I like someone, you know, race shouldn't matter, and they didn't like that. You know, they're like "sellout" crap and stuff like that. [Jason, junior, perceived as black]

Most biracial men voiced resentment and disapproval of the censure many African American women offer them when they date white women. They have difficulty grasping the point of view of black women on this subject. Not one of the biracial men interviewed offered a sympathetic portrayal of why so many African American women are opposed to biracial and black men dating white women. For these biracial men, it just doesn't make sense.

This female freshman who identifies as black voices the concerns of African American women on interracial dating.

I have a lot of color complexes myself, and I don't like to see white girls and black guys. I mean, it's weird when people ask me, "Well you're mixed, why do you feel that way?" And I don't. I guess because I'm so set in being with a black guy, I feel like you're taking one of our men away from us or something like that. [Valerie, freshman, perceived as black]

This idea of "taking one of our men away" is common in the community of African American women. There are far more eligible single black women than marriageable black men.[4] This leads to some resentment on the part of African American women when they see one of the few eligible black men coupling with a white woman.

For those biracial women who identify as black, the situation is a bit more complex. They, like black women, resent what they see as one of their few prospects choosing to date a white woman rather than one of "their own." However, they also have to acknowledge that their very existence was based on an interracial coupling (most likely that of a black male and a white female). Lisa Jones of the *Village Voice*, who is of both African American and white descent, describes her feelings about white-female/black-male couples this way: "These duos tangle up my emotions; I look at them as a child of an interracial marriage, but also as a black woman who has witnessed the market value put on white femininity" [Jones, 1994]. It is no wonder that Jones's emotions are "tangled up." So, too, are those of many other biracial women who identify as black.

On the other hand, white friends of biracial college students also have their own expectations for whom their biracial friend(s) should date. They often assume that the biracial individual will date black people or biracial people if available.

There's one guy on campus that we've become good friends with, and he's black and everyone sees him and they're like, "Oh, you guys would make the best couple." It's like, "Why? Because he's the only black guy you know?" They have no reasoning behind it. And there's another student here who I don't know, but my friend has a class with him and he's also biracial and he said, "There's this guy in my class, he's biracial. You guys would have the cutest kids. You'd have the cutest, you'd be the cutest." And he said, "You'd really like him." I'm like, "I may have nothing in common with this guy," you know. But we would make the "perfect couple." [Julia, freshman, perceived as black]

For many, there are serious repercussions to being perceived as failing the racial litmus test. Some are literally driven from the communities in which they find themselves tested. Brandon, a biracial male who has chosen to avoid such pressures by dating nonwhite women, describes his sister's uncomfortable experience with her racial litmus examination.

My sister chose to go the opposite way. She has been dating, and her boyfriend's white. She's been dating him for over two years now. And the problems that I was foreseeing for me happened to her when she was at Highland College. She transferred from Highland College to State University. I think one of the major reasons why she transferred was because of the hostility that was being directed toward her while she was on campus at Highland. And it was particularly from the black community. "You're black, you're selling out, you're dating this white guy." You know, nasty looks, comments, while she's walking with him. She dealt with all types of things like that. And at one point, I remember her talking to my mother and just saying, "I don't know if I can do this." They were breaking her down, and their relationship was a little bit rocky there for a while, because she couldn't take it. [Brandon, 24, perceived as black]

Brandon's sister chose to transfer out of the college in which she experienced such racial tension. While she is still dating her white boyfriend, the experience has made her examine her own racial identity. She is now much more aware of her African American racial heritage.

Obviously, when it comes to dating, race is still very much an issue for many Americans. Biracial individuals face pressure from both the black and the white community. Ironically, both populations are pulling them in the same direction—toward identifying as black. Our racial structure does not yet allow biracial Americans to choose freely between their two racial heritages. While many have "passed" into white society in history, none were able to do so without breaking ties to the black community and living in constant fear of exposure. Today some biracial Americans are withstanding great pressure and declaring themselves to be both white and black. The racial structure is beginning to crack, but it will not fall without a tremendous struggle.

Many members of the African American community are counting on the biracial person to make the "right" choice and date black people. On the other hand, most white people simply expect that biracial individuals will make the "natural" decision to date their "fellow" African Americans. However, for many biracial college students who have grown up with both a black and a white parent in a predominantly white neighborhood, the choice to date black people is neither "natural" nor necessarily "right" for them. The fact that most[5] of those interviewed have dated white individuals has produced much tension.

CONCLUSION

Biracial individuals still face many racial hurdles they must overcome in the dating world. Unlike most black and white people, the overwhelming majority of biracial persons are exposed to *both* whites and African Americans from the day they are born. Intuitively, many might think that, by having a parent of each race, biracial persons should not have race as a concern when they choose either a dating partner or a mate. While many strive to live out that racial ideal, most are confronted with the harshness of a racially sensitive world. However, as indicated by the college students interviewed here, most young biracial adults are not following the traditional "one drop rule" and dating only black persons.

As a growing number of biracial people define themselves as both black and white, the monoracial people around them must respond to their desire to date both black and white people. It can no longer be assumed that those with African American ancestry will "naturally" marry a black American. The stringent racial structure in the United States is beginning to falter. Indeed, the very acknowledgment of biracial individuals is evidence of that. Through the stories of these biracial college students we can see that many monoracial people are still struggling with this reality. Nevertheless, the freedom these biracial individuals are both demanding and using to date and mate whom they please is proof that the historical racial caste system in the United States is being challenged as never before.

With these changes in patterns of dating and self-definition comes the need to reexamine the question of marginality among biracial persons. As the numbers of biracial Americans increase and the monoracial social definitions of race in the United States are being questioned, it is no longer clear that Robert Park's famous declaration of black-white Americans as "marginal" still holds true. The next chapter examines whether or not Park's definition of marginality applies to biracial Americans today.

NOTES

1. In the cases of those interviewed, these colleges were predominantly white. No interviewee was attending an all-black institution when interviewed.

2. As Mariah P. P. Root [1992:5] explains, "subsequently, multiracial people experience a 'squeeze of oppression' *as* people of color and *by* people of color."

3. This acceptance by many African American males of black men dating white women has existed since at least the Civil Rights and Black Power movements. Especially during the early to mid-1960s when Civil Rights organizations were integrated, black male activists and white female activists often established romantic relationships with one another. While many of these relationships were based on mutual love and affection, others were more of a political statement than a personal relationship. For some white women, it was a means of "proving" they were not racist. For some black men, having a sexual relationship with a white woman "proved" his manhood and equality with, or even superiority over, white men. Many African American women in Civil Rights and black nationalist organizations found that their potential black mates were ignoring them and focusing their romantic and sexual interests on white women [see Evans, 1979:88–90 and Wallace, 1979:3–33].

4. According to Russell et al. in *The Color Complex* [1992], "in some areas there are as many as eight marriageable Black women for every marriageable Black man, and during the past twenty years the incidence of Black marriages has dropped by 20 percent." Russell et al. point out that this scarcity of marriageable black males is due in large part to high rates of unemployment, incarceration, and violence among African American men.

5. See chart on page 129.

5
Marginality and the Biracial American

As the increasing population of black-white mixed-race persons challenges the prevailing racial structure, we must reexamine traditional sociological beliefs concerning biracial Americans. The most famous sociological concept applied to these persons has been marginality. Robert Park [1928] constructed the definition of "marginal" persons almost seventy years ago.

In the introduction to E. V. Stonequist's *Marginal Man* [1937/1961:xiiii], Park defines a marginal man as "one whom fate has condemned to live in two societies and in two, not merely different, but antagonistic cultures." The marginal person is doomed to live as a stranger in both these worlds. He or she is from, but not of, two very distinct societies. It is important to note, however, that because of their separateness from both of their ancestral societies, marginal persons have a "wider horizon, keener intelligence, [and] more detached and rational viewpoint" than "full" members of either group. While the marginal man or woman may, personally, crave a sense of belonging, their view of society is unique and broader than that of nonmarginal persons.

In defining marginality, Park discusses a concept that is rooted in classical theory but also has been utilized recently in works such as feminist critiques. Georg Simmel examined marginality in his examination of the "stranger." In many ways, Simmel's stranger is akin to Park's marginal person. The stranger is part of a group, but not yet a full member of it. However, "by virtue of his partial involvement in group affairs he can obtain an objectivity that other members cannot reach" [Coser, 1977:182].

Both Simmel and Park refer to the stereotypical wandering Jew as, respectively, the typical "stranger" or "marginal" person. According to Park, "most if not all the characteristics of the Jew, certainly his pre-eminence as a trader and his keen intellectual interest, his sophistication, his idealism and lack of historic sense," and his nomadic life are all "characteristics . . . [of] the cosmopolite" [Park,

1928:891]. Before the creation of the state of Israel after World War II, Jewish persons had no homeland to call their own. They were residents of many lands but accepted as full members by none, hence their marginalization.

Park believed that those of mixed-race descent were also marginal. He maintained that biracial Americans and Eurasians, in particular, are the quintessential marginal persons. Members of both these groups "live in two worlds, in both of which [they are] more or less stranger[s]" [Park, 1928:893]. Both persons live in societies in which friction and obvious physical distinctions exist between their parents' racial groups.

Sandra Harding's description of feminist standpoint epistemology mirrors aspects of Park's marginal person. Female researchers who begin from this form of epistemology use their position as outsiders in the predominantly patriarchal society to obtain a more complete picture of how society functions. Just as marginal people have a "wider horizon" and more "detached and rational viewpoint" due to their unique position, "women researchers are 'outsiders within' . . . whose standpoints promise to enrich sociological discourse" [Harding, 1991:131]. In effect, any group that has been marginalized in society (e.g., single fathers, homosexuals, illiterate persons, racial/ethnic minorities) can contribute insights about our society not found in mainstream, dominant culture.

There are two primary aspects of marginality: (1) feeling unable to "fit in"—being from, but not of, two exclusive societies and (2) having a more objective or "cosmopolitan" view of society than monoracial Americans. This chapter examines whether young biracial Americans manifest these characteristics of marginality. I will first explore how the attempts of biracial Americans, born immediately before the Civil Rights Movement, to avoid the fate of marginality contrast with the experiences of younger biracial persons. As we will see, avoiding marginality is as much a product of social evaluation as becoming marginal. Marginality, like race, is socially defined. Just as race is socially determined, so are marginal persons.

BIRACIAL IDENTITY AND MARGINALITY BEFORE AND AFTER THE CIVIL RIGHTS MOVEMENT

Before the Civil Rights Movement, and the subsequent multicultural movement, persons who were clearly the offspring of both white and black parents were susceptible to the fate of marginality. The only way they could avert this destiny was if the black community overlooked the white racial heritage and embraced the biracial person as one of its own. While still possible, this situation grew more complicated if the white parent of the biracial person lived with the rest of the family. In cases like this, the African American community often adopted the white parent as an honorary black person. In turn, the entire family embraced African American culture. Barbara, a forty-eight-year-old interviewee, described just such a process in her own family. Her white mother relinquished her white identity when she married Barbara's father.

Barbara's family also illustrates the inability of one biracial person to assimilate into the African American community. Her brother Bob's life is a powerful portrait of what happened to many biracial persons who were rejected by the black community. Although he had a black father, Bob did not appear as though he had any African heritage. His childhood was a miserable one, filled with constant taunts from African American neighbors. Bob's social awkwardness and white appearance earned him only enmity from black persons. During his childhood, there was little he could do about the situation. As an adult, Bob fled both his black surroundings and his African American heritage. He "passed" and became white. In neither the black nor the white community was it possible for him to embrace publicly both sides of his racial heritage. In order to survive and avoid marginalization, he had to choose between the two. Rejected by the black community because of his mannerisms and appearance, Bob's only alternative was to become white.

Susan shares a story similar to Barbara's in terms of society's influence over her racial self-definition. She, however, grew up as a member of the one "Negro family" in their predominantly white neighborhood. In determining the race of the family, Susan's neighbors never acknowledged her Caucasian mother's foreign background and her biracial heritage. Susan did not believe she had any choice but to identify as exclusively black. While Susan's light appearance sometimes forces her to explain her black identity to persons with whom she interacts, her strong and unwavering identity as African American has enabled her to fit into the black community and avoid one of the typical issues of marginality.

Unlike Barbara's brother, Barbara and Susan were able to find acceptance in the African American community. It was clear to them that this was necessary to ensure survival in racially divided pre-Civil Rights America. They never attempted to claim a biracial identity.

On the other hand, two-thirds of this study's biracial interviewees born after 1965 *do* maintain biracial identities. They actively attempt to straddle the racial divide. In doing so, they are prime candidates for the role and experience of marginal persons, if Park's concept of marginality were still applicable today. The truth is more complicated. It is no longer possible to declare unequivocally that all biracial persons are doomed to "live in . . . two antagonistic societies."

As discussed in Chapter 3, the United States is increasingly becoming a multiracial, rather than a monoracial, society. While there was always some racial diversity in the United States, the extent of the diversity is greater than ever. Statistics indicate that European Americans will be a minority in this nation by the year 2060 ["The Numbers Game," Fall 1993:12]. Europe, once the main exporter of immigrants to the United States, now gives birth to a mere 10 percent of those entering this nation. The remaining 90 percent come predominantly from nations of people of color. Mexico, the Philippines, Cuba, Korea, China, and Taiwan are now the six largest contributors of new immigrants [Weisberger, 1994]. Moreover, as previously mentioned, interracial marriages are increasing.

As a result of the structural and cultural changes in society highlighted in Chapter 3, the United States is now a relatively more welcome place for biracial persons than it was thirty years ago. While the older interviewees have more mixed interpretations of their experiences as biracial persons, the vast majority of the under-thirty interviewees are happy they have a mixed-race background. Most of the thirty-two younger interviewees recognize both positive and negative consequences to having both a black and a white parent, but all but two believe the positive aspects outweigh the negative. There is a marked difference in how older and younger biracial adults deal with marginalization. Few biracial persons under the age of thirty attempt to avoid exposing half of their racial heritage. In all cases, racial appearance plays a large role in determining the pressures biracial persons face and the acceptance they garner from the larger society. It also affects the degree of marginalization biracial persons encounter.

INFLUENCE OF APPEARANCE ON MARGINALIZATION

As discussed in Chapter 4, racial appearance is critical in determining how persons of both races react toward a biracial person. It is extremely difficult to maintain an identity not supported by those with whom we interact. It is often difficult for biracial men and women who appear either black or white to convince people that they have both an African American and a white parent. Biracial persons who appear neither white nor black have a greater opportunity to define their own identity and to have a mixed racial identity supported, or at least recognized, by the larger society. John, who appears mixed, understands this.

Because there is such ambiguity in how I look, I have a lot of freedom to create my own self-perception. If I was darker, then it would be set. I would have felt more inclined to toe the line and define as black. Similarly, if I looked white, I'd probably be more inclined to define as white. [John, 30, perceived as Italian/mixed]

John maintains that his ambiguous racial appearance allows him to create and maintain his identity as a mixed racial person. It enables him to derive some support for his biracial identity from persons with whom he interacts.

Racial appearance that is neither black nor white can also lead to a fluid racial identity. As mentioned in Chapter 3, the importance of racial appearance (as contrasted with known ascribed status) in determining racial identity grows as the United States becomes a more mobile and urban-centered society. It is increasingly easy for biracial persons who are neither clearly white nor black to change their racial self-definition from one situation to the next. They experience having their identity perceived differently in separate situations—a situation rare for previous generations. Some biracial persons with ambiguous racial features also find themselves defined by others in numerous different ways. Phillip, one of the youngest interviewees, is a good example of such a person.

There was a period where others defined me for me. When I skateboarded I was white, when I surfed I was white, when I boogey-boarded I was white, when I played soccer I was white, and when I played baseball I was white. When I played football, I was a black kid. When I played basketball, I was a black kid. When I was angry and went out jacking people, I was a black kid. That's the way they looked at me. I was young and vulnerable, so that's the way I saw myself as well. It kind of bends like that. It's really true. I mean it flips you out [laughs]. [Phillip, 18, perceived as a Caribbean Islander]

At another point in his life, Phillip himself used his appearance to alter his identity to one more palatable to the racial groups surrounding him. During his early childhood in a Puerto Rican and black inner-city neighborhood, he learned quickly the benefits of having a malleable racial identity.

I got beat up by black kids for being half-white. I started saying, "No, no, no. I'm Puerto Rican. I'm Puerto Rican. I'm Puerto Rican." And then, next thing I know, it's all cool because of the fact that my uncle married a Puerto Rican woman. Another uncle of mine married a Puerto Rican. So that's two different sets of interbreeding and families, Puerto Ricans, blacks, till it's all Puerto Rican. . . . I'm Puerto Rican. [Phillip, 18, perceived as a Caribbean Islander]

Not only did Phillip change his declaration of racial identity, he actually began to believe that he was Puerto Rican instead of black and white. Supported by his Puerto Rican relatives and his ambiguous racial features, Phillip became Puerto Rican. He was able to establish a compromise racial category, neither white nor black, that was acceptable to his neighbors.

As a child moving to a predominantly minority inner-city neighborhood, Phillip managed to adapt his racial identity to fit his changing needs. However, it is not necessarily easy to deal with having multiple racial identities. Neither is it simple to maintain a single biracial identity when society still upholds a monoracial racial structure.

Some biracial persons wish they were simply either black or white. They neither crave nor savor the battle to dismantle the present racial structure. Yolanda is one such person.

I wish I were one way or the other. I wish I were all black so I could just know that I'm a black person or I were all white so I could just be a white person. But since I'm neither, it makes it harder because I have to be Yolanda. Maybe everybody should just be who they are instead of what their race is. . . . But being both black and white means a part of your identity is not established. [Yolanda, 18, perceived as black]

While Yolanda recognizes the ideal that race should not figure in a person's identity, she suffers through the reality that race still matters in the United States. She also realizes that identity is partially dependent upon group membership.

The white side is probably truer to who I am. Probably because I was raised by Mom, who is white. I think that has a lot to do with it. And I was always in white neighborhoods and with white kids. That's what did it for me. That sealed my fate [slight laugh]. I have a friend in Tennessee who's also biracial. She lives two doors down the street from my grandmother. We've known each other since we were two, and she lived with both her parents, but she lives in a black neighborhood and went to black schools and she's "down." And I think that's because she had more black influence growing up. Although I'm definitely aware of my blackness, I feel more white than black because my background was white. [Yolanda, 18, perceived as white]

As noted in Chapter 3, the majority of the under-thirty interviewees who racially identify as black grew up in predominantly minority neighborhoods. Yolanda is similar to most young biracial persons raised in largely white residential areas. Even though her black racial appearance requires her to inform others of her biracial background, she does, though, steadfastly identify as both black and white. She may wish that she were born either one or the other, but having been born as both, she maintains an identity as a biracial person even though she realizes that this is not an "established" identity. She takes comfort in the fact that she is a "child of love"—the product of two people who had to overcome obstacles to be together because society disapproved of their relationship. The knowledge of her parent's triumph over racial adversity gives her strength when she feels marginalized.

One of the negative aspects of being biracial Yolanda must face is not being able to always "fit in" easily with either blacks or whites. As described in Chapter 4, almost every interviewee under thirty spoke of feeling "not black enough around black people and not white enough around white people." This is a major effect of marginalization.

NOT FITTING IN

Many biracial persons, raised in upper middle-class, predominantly white neighborhoods, find they have little in common with African Americans they meet who live in different areas and on a lower socioeconomic level. Stacy, while perceived as black, discovered she came from a completely different culture than her black female classmates.

I had really bad experiences with black women. And I didn't fit in. I wasn't from the same neighborhood. I lived in a different part of town. Our parents did different things. We didn't go to the same churches. We didn't know much about one another. [Stacy, 18, perceived as black]

Stacy's long, straight hair added to the tension. She believes her female African American classmates coveted her "good" hair and resented her economic class and success in school.

Other interviewees discussed feeling "different" from those around them because of their biracial background. One compared herself and her brother to "aliens."

My brother and I have talked about sort of just feeling different from most everybody we're around [laughs]. He has a friend, she's actually a Japanese woman, and she met him at a gym, and they talked about how they both sort of feel like aliens. This woman said that she knew when she met him that he was an alien like she was. She's just different. She's not like most of the other people in her family and in her culture. And she could tell that he was kind of an alien too. It's hard to describe. It's kind of like being alone and not really a part of a real cohesive larger group. Not having a real clan, like a big clan, that you are a part of. [Kim, 33, perceived as black]

Kim's use of the word "alien" is indicative of her feeling separate and apart from others. Persons often employ the word alien to describe outsiders and foreigners—classic marginal persons. While comfortable with her identity as both black and biracial, Kim nevertheless finds herself yearning for a large family that shares her racial background. She wishes to find a place where she truly feels at home.

Some young biracial persons find themselves with a constant sense of being an "outsider." Again, this is symptomatic of marginality. This sense of nonbelonging is especially evident among interviewees who, while encouraged by their parents to embrace both sides of their racial heritage, grew up in primarily white environments where there were few, if any, other interracial families. Gloria, whose parents taught her to appreciate both her black and her white racial heritage, is typical of such persons. Surrounded by predominantly white people at home, she always felt somewhat different from those around her. When she attended college and interacted with black students, she sensed that she was also not quite like them.

I sort of have defined myself as not part of things—as sort of something else—because I've never really been in a group or in an environment where I'm with other people whose parents are mixed like mine. So I guess I've always felt sort of like an outsider in that sense, and I really don't see that as something that's going to change because it informed so much of my growing up. [Gloria, 20, perceived as white]

This sense of separateness is similar to what inspired Valerie's childhood desire to know where she "fit." As a child who looked like neither one of her parents, she was unsure to which racial group she belonged.

I knew my mother was white, my father was black, and I was a brown child—and I didn't look much like either one of them. I wasn't the complexion of my father, nor was I the complexion of my mother. It's been a lot of different stages, but as a child I did have a kind of problem with identity and knowing which side I really fit in and who was accepting me. Kids can be cruel, and I remember people would say, "What are you? Where do you fit in?" [Valerie, 18, perceived as black]

Raised in a diverse and lower middle-class neighborhood, Valerie eventually decided she should identify as black. She said her father reminding her that she was "another nigger just like him and her grandmother" strongly influenced her racial self-definition.

Not looking like their parents was a concern raised by many interviewees besides Valerie. College student Cheryl spoke of how important it was for her that people realize that she belonged with her parents. She is very grateful for a younger sister who looks very much like her. Biracial persons without siblings are part of a family the general public does not easily recognize as a family. This raises many issues of belonging with which biracial individuals must deal.

Many times, monoracial persons blatantly insult a biracial child because of his or her racial appearance, further underscoring the feeling that they don't fit in. One interviewee, raised in all-black neighborhoods where he stood out due to his light skin color, remembers having to choose between two racially derogative labels for himself.

I remember once I was at my dad's house and I went out to the playground to play. This [black] guy who was there said, "Damn!" Like he couldn't believe me when he laid his eyes on me. "Damn shorty. Are you a honky or a nigger?" I didn't know what a honky was, but I knew a nigger was something bad. So, I said "I'm a honky." And he goes, "I'm a honky too." Just mocking me. I mean, I just felt like people were just going to attack me if I walked down the street. [Joel, 23, perceived as Latino]

Life as a light-skinned boy who possesses the stereotypical attributes of whiteness, such as speaking proper English and being a serious student, was not easy for Joel in his African American urban neighborhood. In high school, black classmates called him "white boy" and attacked him several times. Currently a graduate student, it was not until he attended a prestigious college with a small black population that he felt accepted as an African American. More comfortable with his biracial heritage now, Joel describes himself as mixed racial.

Jason has faced rejection from both black and white persons. Perceived as black, he has been disparaged by white supremacists who view him as black and by African Americans who disapprove of his biracial identity.

I've been rejected by both sides. I felt the intolerance and the insensitivity of people and what a big emphasis people put on color. People take a look at color before they look at you as a person. I think that I've noticed that maybe more than other people have. A lot of the black people here say that black people can't be racist cause they don't have power, whatever. I can personally say that I don't agree with that. Cause I've seen it and I've experienced it. I think there's intolerance all over this society. All people are intolerant. I think everyone's racist in some way or another. I think I've come to realize that through all the things I've been through. [Jason, 20, perceived as black]

Clearly, Jason's experience has encouraged his negative perception of society.

Park's definition of marginality resonates in these examples of problems with assimilation. These stories describe situations in which biracial persons lack a sense of belonging. In a still predominantly monoracial society, there is no set place for biracial Americans.[1] While society has changed to the point that the majority of mixed-race persons choose to define themselves racially as biracial, aspects of marginality still exist. Biracial Americans possess the positive as well as the negative attributes of marginality, however. Almost all the interviewees spoke enthusiastically about the benefits of a biracial background.

THE GIFT OF OBJECTIVITY

Many of the interviewees' positive comments reflect Park's idea that marginal men and women "offer a more detached and rational viewpoint" than do monoracial persons. The ability to have "an open mind" is something every under-thirty interviewee believes comes with a biracial background. Helen's thoughts are typical of this view.

Being biracial has made me different. I think it allows me to see both sides. I think being mixed racial is really unique. I feel really lucky that I am. I am a minority big time [laughing]. But I think it allows me to see things with more of an open mind or more with my eyes open than maybe someone who just comes from one cultural background does. [Helen, 22, perceived as white]

Elizabeth echoes Helen's idea that biracial persons have an open mind. She believes that biracial persons can act as mediators between black and white persons. She spoke of a time she acted in such a role in college.

Biracial persons can work as a liaison between black people and white people. We can enlighten them. When I first went to school I had three roommates, and they were all white. And they were from some country part of Maryland, and they called black people colored. They didn't understand certain things, and I could teach them. They accepted me cause at first they didn't know what I was. They thought I was white, and they would just talk freely and openly. By the time I said, "Do you know I'm black?" they had already befriended me so it was kind of hard for them to say, "Well, now I don't like her because she's black." So it kind of worked as a way for them to learn things and become friends with me and realize, "Oh, I can become friends with a black person. I just realized that she's black and there's nothing wrong with her." And, likewise, with black people you can get them to give white people a chance. Cause a lot of them, especially those from cities, grow up not giving white people any kind of chance. But they became friends with me and my [white] roommates. And they'd come over and visit me and start to talk to my roommates and eventually they said, "All right, you're all right." So they started to open their eyes and say, "Ok, I see. She's white and she's not that bad." [Elizabeth, 25, perceived as Hispanic, nonblack]

The ability to recognize commonalities among races is a recurring theme among the interviewees. Janine also maintains that her racial heritage has enabled her to recognize the similarities between the black and white races.

I think it's positive because it's forced me to see similarities between groups more. My entire life has been focused on synthesizing things. So I think that's greatly shaped who I am. And I tend not to stereotype people as much as. . . . Well, I suppose I do, but it's in a different way. Like anyone who's mixed is automatically OK in my book. So I suppose that's a kind of prejudice that I have [laughing]. But usually I'm more sensitive to people coming from different backgrounds. [Janine, 18, perceived as black]

Other interviewees spoke of how their mixed racial background has prevented them from being racist. Jane maintains that her mixed racial background has allowed her to view others without racial blinders.

I think that having both a black and a white parent has given me the best of both worlds. I think it's given me the ability to accept people for who they are and not look for black or white or use race to discriminate or make judgments of people. It's definitely been positive. I truly feel blessed to be mixed. [Jane, 26, perceived as Hispanic]

While she believes her life would have been easier if she had two white parents, she is grateful for the insights that come, along with the hardships, from being biracial.

Sarah, in a similar vein to Jane, believes that she could never be racist knowing that she is the product of both a black and a white parent.

Being biracial has been definitely positive. *Definitely* positive, because I have a hard time understanding racism. I could never, ever, have a racist view just because of who I am. Because I would feel I wasn't being true to myself. In terms of, you know, black/white issues. I feel I'm more openminded because of that. It also makes me an interesting person. I'm a little bit different. I like it a lot better than if I was just white or if I was just black. [Sarah, 19, perceived as white]

In fact, Sarah says that she never even notices the race of persons with whom she interacts. She strongly believes that her mixed racial background has freed her from the racial blinders most monoracial persons wear. For Sarah, as well as Jane, the positive attributes of being biracial clearly outweigh the negative.

Sybil, another college student, uses a story to illustrate the unique perspective available to biracial persons.

One of my roommates [who's black] was talking with this [black] girl who asked her, "Do you think white people do the same thing on dates?" My roommate just gave her a stupid look like, "Yeah, they do, you fool." And I'm just thinking I've had all these conversations where like white people would say something like that to me or black people would say something like that to me. I don't think a lot of people get the opportunity to know, oh yeah, they do kind of do the same thing. Do you realize how stupid this is? It's just really kind of dumb, this whole prejudice thing. But you even get to see how more stupid it is when you're biracial because when you're biracial everything is seen through different eyes. I mean you can never, ever make absolutes about either race. [Sybil, 20, perceived as black]

Like Jane and Sarah, Sybil maintains that biracial persons are able to see "through different eyes" than monoracial persons. Being racially prejudiced just does not make sense to these young biracial persons. They maintain that it would be impossible for them to be prejudiced against any racial group because they themselves are the product of two traditionally feuding races. These biracial persons are able to see the commonalities between races. As Janine puts it, her "entire life has been focused on synthesizing things." Their very existence cries out against the historic separation and distinction between races.

Even Jason, who has faced rejection from both blacks and whites, believes that being biracial is a good experience. He paraphrases Nietzsche's saying, "whatever doesn't kill you makes you stronger" to describe his feelings about being biracial. His life as a biracial person has helped him to grow and become a more open person.

It has been positive for me. I've learned a lot from it. I've been exposed more than most people to two different cultures. I'm not so closeminded. The exposure I've gotten has really been invaluable. You know, some things will sidetrack you. Like getting name-called and all, that's just a little ignorance. People are going to be ignorant. You just can't let that detract from your experience. [Jason, 20, perceived as black]

Most young biracial adults share Jason's positive perception of having a biracial background. While the older biracial interviewees stressed the hardships of having both a black and a white parent, the vast majority of the interviewees under thirty emphasized the benefits of a mixed-race background.

Like members of any other marginal group, biracial men and women possess a broader and more objective view of society than nonmarginal persons. Those who claim a biracial identity view race and our race-based society in general in a markedly different manner than the average monoracial American. The vast majority of the under-thirty interviewees agree with Park that they are more "cosmopolitan" than non mixed-race persons.

CONCLUSION

Unlike the prevailing view among Park and his contemporaries, and contrary to the experiences of biracial persons born before the Civil Rights Movement, young biracial men and women today believe that the positive attributes of biracial identity outweigh the negative. The fact that escalating numbers of young persons of both black and white racial heritage choose to embrace a biracial identity is evidence of this fact. While they still share many experiences of Park's "marginal man," the implications of marginality have changed. Although many biracial persons today feel like outsiders, there is currently an increasing acceptance of multiracial identity in the United States. Moreover, the positive aspects of marginality remain. Biracial persons believe they "retain a more detached and rational viewpoint" than do monoracial Americans. Today young black-white persons feel not only different but, in some ways, wiser than monoracial persons. The overwhelming majority do not wish they were born any other way.

NOTE

1. This is gradually changing. There are now organizations specifically designed for multiracial persons—such as interracial campus groups and community-based mixed-race support groups—in which biracial persons do "fit in." As discussed in Chapter 4, however,

there are now only a small number of these groups on college campuses nationwide (Harvard, Brown, and Stanford are home to some of the more well known groups). Local groups, while on the rise, are also still in short supply. For instance, the city of Boston, as of 1996, did not have an active mixed-race support group.

6
Identities and Transformation

In order to understand how identity is transformed, it is first necessary to comprehend how identity is initially formed. Much theoretical work has been devoted to the study of identity formation. Sparked by Erik Erikson's [1946] development of the term *ego-identity*, sociologists have been studying the concept of identity for the past five decades. The symbolic interactionist perspective and its theoretical offshoots, in particular, have produced a large number of key works in this area. Some of the most notable are Strauss 1959; McCall and Simmons 1966/1978; Glaser and Strauss 1971; and Stryker 1968, 1980, 1982, 1987, 1992. Postmodern theorists are also grappling with this issue and produce concepts that are relevant to understanding the transformation of racial identity among biracial persons.

This chapter reviews these symbolic interactionist-based works and presents my own application of their insights to the transformation of racial identity among biracial persons. Finally, it provides an analysis of what symbolic interactionists can learn from postmodern theorists concerning the transformation of racial identity and the larger societal emergence of multiple role identities.

THE EARLY SYMBOLIC INTERACTIONIST THEORY OF IDENTITY FORMATION AND TRANSFORMATION

Symbolic interactionism reveals how persons discover their own identity by interacting with other actors through the use of shared gestures and symbols. In the eyes of a symbolic interactionist, the world is "a social construction" [Fine, 1990:138]. Interactions between actors are the force by which society is both maintained and propelled forward. Persons perceive themselves and their roles in society according to how they are viewed by people with whom they interact. It is through communicating with others that persons understand who they are and how they fit into society. For instance, Olympic athletes have no doubt been told by many persons throughout their lives that they are exceptional athletes. This type of recognition enables the athletes to perceive themselves as possible Olympians and encourages them to train extensively in their sport and, in fact, become Olympic athletes.

There is a constant exchange between the self and society. Because humans have minds, they are able to act as well as react. Individuals both are formed by and form society. George Herbert Mead writes that each actor "is continually reacting back against this society. Every adjustment involves some sort of change in the community to which the individual adjusts himself" [Mead, 1934:235]. But if actors perceive themselves and their roles in society by the manner in which they are viewed by those around them, there is not room for much individuality to spring forth. It is also unclear exactly how transformations in group identity occur. Symbolic interactionists have tended to focus on the individual and small group, with insufficient attention to larger societal and structural dynamics. The following works strive to fill this gap in symbolic interactionism.

THE SEARCH FOR IDENTITY AND STATUS PASSAGES

Anselm Strauss's *Mirrors and Masks: The Search for Identity* [1959] prompted symbolic interactionists to make identity a central concern of their field [Weigert et al., 1986:10]. In this work, Strauss stresses the importance of language, interaction, and history on the formation and transformation of identity. He writes that "any name is a container; poured into it are the conscious or unwitting evaluations of the namer" [Strauss, 1959:15]. Names work to fix identities. Altering names indicates "a rite of passage" . . . a "passage" to a "new self-image" [Strauss, 1959:16,17].

While some changes in identity are accompanied by changes in titles (e.g., mother, widow, vice president, manager, teacher, Ph.D.), others are marked by individual name alterations. When Catholics go through the process of confirmation in their faith, they choose a new name for themselves that indicates they are confirmed Catholics. Likewise, traditionally, when couples marry, the woman has taken her husband's last name and discarded her own. A couple sharing the same last name is symbolic of the "rite of passage" from single to married life. The relatively new alternatives of married persons combining both their original last names with hyphens and women simply retaining their maiden names after marriage are indicative of yet another transformation of identity—the growing independence of women from men.

According to Strauss, the naming, or classification of things is constantly in flux. Definitions are never clearly construed. Expectations are never completely met. This uncertainty promotes a need for "reassessment." During this period of reassessment, it is possible to create new definitions of situations. "It is in the areas of ambiguity that transformations take place . . . without such areas transformation would be impossible" [Strauss, 1959:26]. The relatively new ambiguity of what it means to be a married woman is one example of such uncertainty. The increasing number of women who retain their maiden name signifies the increasing uncertainty of the role of wife in our society. No longer is it clear that a wife's obligation is to be a homemaker and a demure and unacknowledged supporter of her husband and children. She is now allowed, expected, or, in many cases, forced to work outside as well as within the home.

Strauss's idea that classification is never constant and is continually being transformed certainly holds true for the racial identity of black-white Americans. Throughout U.S. history, there have been periods when the racial identity of mixed-race people has been ambiguous. This uncertainty led to the creation of new social constructions of who is black and who is white. The creation of the "one drop rule" is the most famous example of such attempts at clarifying racial identity.

The transformation of identity takes place on both the individual and the societal level. All persons experience a change in their self-identity at various points throughout their life. Graduations, marriages, and job loss are all examples of ritual or rite of passage events during which persons tend to reevaluate themselves. The same occurrence that spurs on a change in identity in one individual is "extremely likely to befall and to be equally significant to other persons of the same generation, occupation, and social class" [Strauss, 1959:100]. For instance, the Civil Rights Movement affected not only the self-conception of certain black individuals, but the identity of the whole generation of black Americans.

"Personal identity is meshed with group identity, which rests upon an historical past" [Strauss, 1959:173]. The history of biracial Americans described in Chapters 1 and 4 led to the transformation of racial identity in the newest generation of black-white adults. The majority of young biracial individuals now racially define themselves as biracial, rather than exclusively black. According to Strauss, "a concern with . . . personal identities requires a serious parallel concern with shared, or collective identities, viewed through time" [Strauss:175]. It is the change in how individual black-white Americans racially define themselves that leads us to examine how the latest generation of those with both a black and a white parent identify themselves racially.

In *Status Passages* [1971], Barney Glaser joins Strauss in outlining a formal theory of "transitions" that clearly germinated in *Mirrors and Masks*. In the more recent work, Glaser and Strauss concentrate on the movement of persons from one status to another. As discussed in *Mirrors and Masks*, everyone travels through several "status passages" during a lifetime.

Status passages may be generated in two ways—chartered or emergent. Chartered passages are the result of a planned and negotiated passage, while emergent passages are formed as they occur. Emergent passages, once routinized, become chartered passages. Becoming a licensed automobile driver is an example of a chartered passage. In each state, there is a specific manner in which one qualifies to receive his or her license. Typically, at the age of fifteen or sixteen, one takes driving lessons, and then passes both a written and a driving test in order to receive a license. Most chartered passages were once emergent. For instance, when cars were first invented, there was no established licensing process. Over the years, however, the passage from a nondriver to a licensed driver became formalized. Other, completely different spheres, such as health (moving from sickness to health) and career (moving from assistant to executive editor), also involve status passages.

The transformation of racial identity among black-white Americans is a type of status passage. It both reflects and contributes to the present changes in the social structure in the United States [Glaser and Strauss, 1971:3]. Race, while connected to phenotypes, is socially defined based upon the prevailing social structure [McCall and Simmons, 1966/1978:29]. As identities become more fluid, this movement is reflected in the transformation of racial identity among biracial persons. When the racial definition of black-white Americans moves from black to biracial, the transformation is both the result of and leads to further alterations in the social structure.

Many of the properties of status passages outlined by Glaser and Strauss [1971:4,5][1] are paralleled in the transformation of racial identity. The transformation is considered desirable by some, undesirable by others, inevitable according to some, while others believe it can be halted and even reversed, and if reversed it could be repeated. It is occurring through the passage of single persons, an aggregate, and a growing collective. Many biracial individuals have simultaneously decided to define themselves as both black and white. As levels of communication and solidarity among black-white Americans increase, biracial persons form biracial support groups that encourage and aid in the transformation process

While the transformation is voluntary so far and not forced by any type of official power source, it is affected by the various levels of control individual biracial persons have over their formation of and identification with their racial identity. Those who are in the upper classes, have parents who encourage them to acknowledge both sides of their racial heritage, and live in mixed or white neighborhoods have an easier access to a biracial identity than other biracial persons. Those who are raised in poor, predominantly minority neighborhoods by parents who urge them to recognize only their black background will most likely believe they have no real choice in their racial definition.

These immediate influences are especially critical because the transformation is not yet legitimated by government officials (e.g., the Census). While the transformation process is clear to some Americans, it is hazy to others, especially those who are not aware of the existence of biracial persons. Although the transformation is of central importance to some biracial persons, it is of limited interest to others. Finally, in any event, the future existence of a biracial racial identity is uncertain as increasing numbers of the offspring of interracial marriages have their own children [Glaser and Strauss, 1971:86].

Currently the passage of black-white Americans from black to biracial is emergent. If and when the group of mixed racial Americans becomes more cohesive and gains enough power to alter the existing racial structure effectively, a form of multiracial passage will become chartered. It is important to note that this passage will be directed for multiracial, rather than merely biracial, persons. As time progresses, multiracial persons will always outnumber biracial individuals. Most likely, the chartered passage will consist of mixed-race Americans feeling free to choose their racial identity. It will then become routine for Americans with mixed racial backgrounds to have racial identities that are not necessarily obvious to the general public.

Certain persons may *"try 'everything' to halt an undesirable passage"* [Glaser and Strauss, 1971:16].[2] There are foes of interracial marriage and the transformation who are now attempting to halt any further mixing of the races. One prominent example is Hulond Humphries, the former Wedowee, Alabama high school principal who threatened to cancel the 1994 spring prom if interracial couples attended it. In his remarks concerning his decision, he called the black-white biracial girl who protested the cancellation a "mistake." While his decision sparked protests, it is clear that in spite, or because, of his racial views, he has a large number of supporters. In June 1996, he won the Democratic nomination for superintendent of schools. There is no Republican nominee, so voting for Humphries in the Democratic primary was, in effect, a vote to elect him to office ["Alabama Principle in Prom Strife Wins Election," *Boston Globe*, 7/27/96:A15]. The large number of persons who voted for Humphries indicates that there are many people who wish to reverse the transformation process.

Glaser and Strauss explain that "reversibility in a status passage comes from two general sometimes interrelated sources—structural conditions and personal conditions" [Glaser and Strauss, 1971:21]. Whereas the decision of principal Humphries to cancel the prom is an example of the latter, Susan's predictions of a second post-Reconstruction period is an example of structurally based reversibility.

During Reconstruction, we had more interracial marriages; but what happened was, eventually, when the society was under stress, families chose that they were either going to be black or white. . . . Those are the kinds of things people do to survive. To make those kinds of choices, if you were to get through whatever the society is oppressing people about. I don't know that that won't happen again. That's one of the things that makes me nervous about the biracial movement. [Lucy, 46, perceived as white]

Throughout U.S. history, economic hard times have led to racial tensions and a reversion to clear delineations between black and white. According to Susan, it is conceivable that current economic tensions could lead to the reversibility of the transformation.

"The strategic question about the desirability of a passage is *'from whose viewpoint the passage is desirable or undesirable'*" [Glaser and Strauss, 1971:89]. Some blacks are not proponents of the status passage of black-white persons moving from black to biracial. For instance, many well-known minority organizations oppose the idea of multiracial categories. The U.S. Census Bureau has received letters from the National Association for the Advancement of Colored

People, the Urban League, Asian and American Indian groups, and the National Council of La Raza opposing the proposal. Their primary concern is that "their numbers would be diminished by people who check off a multiracial box" [Smith, 6/2/96:A24]. This would affect numerous federal programs such as those that assist minority businesses, prevent excess environmental pollution in minority neighborhoods, assure fairness in mortgage lending, and apportion legislative districts based on numbers of minority voters [Mathews, 7/6/96:A1].[3]

These minority groups are also concerned about the possible dilution of their power in identity membership. They fear they will lose their ability to self-defend their interests if increasing numbers of their population become assimilated into multiracial or even, perhaps, white society. These organizations maintain that the biracial person's minority identity should dominate his or her hierarchy of racial identities.

Strauss's "rite of passage" concept illuminates much of the transformation of racial identity among biracial persons. His idea that identities are constantly in flux is supported by the racial history of black-white Americans. His theory enables us to put the present transformation in both historical and societal contexts. The racial identity of biracial persons has fluctuated throughout the history of the United States. Moreover, theirs is not the only identity that is fluid. As identities become increasingly permeable, it behooves us to reflect upon Strauss's supposition that language, interaction, and history both form and transform identities.

Strauss's and Glazer's work on status passages is also useful in an analysis of the transformation. The change in racial identity among black-white Americans resembles, in process, the status passages that Strauss and Glazer outline. Unfortunately, due most likely to the time period in which they wrote, these theorists never acknowledge that traditionally ascribed identities, such as race, which they refer to as a "master status," could ever be altered. Their sociological analysis reflects a time in which social identities, such as race, were static.[4] Therefore, their work is limited to the more traditional, and perhaps mundane, passages that most persons traverse (e.g., getting a job, receiving a promotion, getting married). The role-identity model, while helpful in other areas, also suffers from this weakness.

THE ROLE-IDENTITY MODEL

The role-identity model, which is another offshoot of the interactionist approach, is described in the seminal work *Identities and Interactions* by George J. McCall and J. L. Simmons [1966/1978]. Role-identity "may be defined as the character and the role that an individual devises for himself as an occupant of a particular social position. . . . [It] is usually rather idealized" [McCall and Simmons, 1966/1978:65]. A person's primary objective is to find support for and "legitimate" these idealized role-identities [McCall and Simmons, 1966/1978:69].

McCall and Simmons point out that identities are not useful merely for those who claim them. Persons are required to have an identity in our society. For instance, in order to know how to react to an approaching male stranger, one has to be able to identify him. Persons will actually force an identity on an unknown who does not define himself or herself. "In mobile, pluralistic societies like our own . . . stereotypes attached to social identities are typically our sole source of orientation toward the majority of people we encounter. From visible clues to social identity, we connect strangers with stereotypes, so that we may predict their behavior and characteristics" [McCall and Simmons, 1966/1978:113].

In our society, an elderly white man in a suit will garner a very different reaction than a young black man in shabby clothing. Stereotypes tell us that the former is harmless while the latter may be potentially harmful. Simply put, "our bodies get in the way of other people, and they have to identify us before they can know what to do to get past us" [McCall and Simmons, 1966/1978:70]. When we come to interact personally with the old man and the youth, however, we may identify them in a more refined way. We may learn that the elderly man is the patriarch of a powerful mob, while the young man is a gifted college student who just completed some volunteer work.

In any event, both men's claims of identity have to be supported by those with whom they interact. "Identity, like freedom, must be won and rewon every day. Each identity must continually be legitimated" [McCall and Simmons, 1966/1978:163]. We need role support, "a set of reactions and performances by others the expressive implications of which tend to confirm one's detailed and imaginative view of himself as an occupant of a position" [McCall and Simmons, 1966/1978:71].

Clearly, however, there is never a perfect correlation between one's self-identity and one's perceived identity. Identities can ebb and flow depending upon the response they receive. Those that receive the most support will gain prominence, while those that are demeaned or ignored will become less conspicuous [McCall and Simmons, 1966/1978:77]. For instance, the white identity of biracial persons is likely to become low on their identity hierarchy if they live in all-black environments, appear black, are treated as exclusively black, constantly hear derogatory statements about white people from their friends, and are personally discriminated against by the few white people with whom they do interact. Persons' identities are comprised of the past reactions they have received from others. These past responses affect their present identity, which in turn determines the reactions of others, which then affects their future identity [McCall and Simmons, 1966/1978:20].

In true interactionist mode, McCall and Simmons declare that persons are both the products of the past and purveyors of the future. "Almost from the beginning he *interacts with*, rather than merely responds to, his environment, and he exerts influences upon the very forces that influence him so greatly" [McCall and Simmons, 1966/1978:202]. The life of a society is similar; today's society is influenced by that of the past and will in turn influence the society of the future.

According to McCall and Simmons, each person has an identity set that develops into an "ever-shifting *hierarchy* of role-identities" [McCall and Simmons, 1966/1978:217]. Those role-identities that are most highly rewarded by those closest to the individual rise to the top of the hierarchy, while those which are discouraged drift to the bottom. Thus parents' encouragement of their children's racial identity is very important. Children of both a black and a white parent are very likely to follow the cues of their parents when deciding whether they will define themselves as either biracial or black. For instance, if parents stress the importance of being black, while they discourage the idea of their being white, their white heritage will play a very small role in their biracial offspring's racial self-conception.

When biracial students go to college and are confronted with expectations from both black and white students to identify as black, they may start to explore their black heritage more and increasingly identify as black. College, for most students, is an identity crucible. Away from home, and spending all their time with new people, they are able to create new identities for themselves. As McCall and Simmons describe, "when one changes his web of face-to-face interactions, he changes himself as well, in the sense that different combinations and contents of role-identities are called forth through interaction" [McCall and Simmons, 1966/1978:220]. If biracial students are treated as black by professors and students alike, their role-identity as black may rise to the top of their role-identity hierarchy.

However, even if the larger society defines them as black, biracial persons who appear black may not necessarily identify themselves as black. As described in Chapter 4, persons are not mere products of their culture. The family is the "gatekeeper." "The family selects, adapts, modifies, and interprets those aspects of the culture or subculture it is aware of and concerned with" [McCall and Simmons, 1966/1978:32]. Clearly, the families of biracial Americans born during the Civil Rights Movement who encouraged their children to identify as both black and white rather than follow the traditional "one drop rule" were adopting the norms of the racial subculture with which they were aware and concerned.

Today "the fading of provincialism and traditionalism, along with the proliferation of subcultural variations, has given the individual more alternatives (and ambiguities) in role models and values" [McCall and Simmons, 1966/1978:33]. Persons have more freedom to choose whom they will be. With increasing alternatives come demands for self-determination. For instance, simple awareness of the possibility of choice in racial identity leads many Americans to want that freedom. Relative deprivation is at work. Biracial Americans born before the Movement did not experience the potentiality of being socially acknowledged as anything but black. Most of today's young black-white persons perceive a growing freedom to identify racially as they please and demand recognition of both sides of their racial heritage. Today's unrest among biracial Americans is based on the gains both black and mixed-race Americans attained in the previous generation. It is only now as black-white Americans experience the hard-won gains of the Civil Rights Movement, and the multicultural and identity group movements, that they realize they might actually choose their own racial identity.

McCall and Simmons provide us with a strong analysis of the influence of relationships on one's identity. They stress, even more than do Glaser and Strauss, the importance of the reaction of those with whom we interact on our identity. Although they do not address it, is easy to apply these ideas to racial identity formation and transformation among biracial Americans. The fact that most young black-white persons who grow up in minority communities identify as black, while the majority of those who are raised in predominantly white communities define themselves as biracial is testimony to the influence of peers on one's identity. Likewise, McCall's and Simmons's concept of the family as the "gatekeeper" also rings true. How the parents of biracial persons racially define their children has a strong influence on how black-white individuals racially define themselves.

Unfortunately, McCall's and Simmons's work cannot be utilized effectively in an analysis of the transformation of racial identity because it is simply too dated. While, as noted above, sections of it can be applied to the transformation, their identity theory, as a whole, must be revised in order to deal adequately with the current fluidity of identity in society today. When McCall and Simmons discuss the growing "alternatives (and ambiguities) in role models and values" they come close to recognizing the present reality of multiple and changing identities. If they were writing *Identities and Interactions* today, they most assuredly would address the present ambiguity of what they determined to be static identities. Last published almost twenty years ago, this groundbreaking book needs to be updated once again.

During the period in which McCall and Simmons first published *Identities and Interactions* [1966], other interactionists were also improving upon and refining the symbolic interactionist perspective. When they discuss the fading of provincialism and the increasing persuasiveness of subcultures, McCall and Simmons hint at the power of social structure on identity. Sheldon Stryker's identity theory gives the environmental forces to which McCall and Simmons refer their legitimate due.

IDENTITY THEORY

Identity theory, a structural form of symbolic interactionism that Sheldon Stryker formulated in the late 1960s, specifically addresses and rectifies some of the shortcomings of symbolic interactionism. It emphasizes the influence of social structure. Symbolic interactionist theorists tend to concentrate on face-to-face interaction while ignoring the constraining influences of social structure. Identity theory's main focus "revolve[s] around choices made in situations in which alternative courses of action are available and reasonable to the person" [Stryker, 1982:205]. The social structure within which persons interact influences what they will decide to do. Identity theorists maintain that persons mirror a "complexly differentiated and organized society" by having "multiple selves" [Stryker, 1982:206]. Whichever self or identity they invoke is influenced by the particular social structure in which they exist.

Stryker maintains that forces such as "community organization [and] class structure" largely determine with whom persons develop relationships. The persons with whom they relate affect the identities they use most often. For instance, if persons are close friends with upper middle-class, well-educated people who share their love of history, they will often utilize their identity as historians. This, in turn, will influence their actions [1987:89]. They may become Civil War reenactors because all their friends are and encourage them to do so as well. The class background of the historians is important because persons' class background affects in which neighborhood they are raised, which determines whom their peers will be, which influences how they perceive and identify themselves, which determines what they will do in life. Unless the historians above are economically comfortable, they would be unable to finance the thousands of dollars needed to outfit themselves in appropriate Civil War uniforms. Likewise, a high degree of education is necessary to develop a great enough interest in the Civil War to prompt someone to become a reenactor.

Persons have as many identities as they do sets of relationships. A person may maintain the identities of friend, foe, basketball player, teacher, and poet, "all of which collectively make up her self" [Stryker, 1982:206,207]. When given a choice, persons will act out the role[5] that fits the identity they assume in a given situation. In all cases, structural elements affect the choice of the individual.

If a biracial woman's social network consists largely of black persons who believe that she should identify as only black, she most likely will. Her identity as black will be extremely salient. This is true of those biracial individuals born before the Civil Rights Movement. As noted in Chapter 3, however, most young biracial adults have been raised in predominantly white neighborhoods. The majority of them were taught by their parents to identify as both black and white. The most common area in which their biracial identity has been challenged is on racial classification forms.

During epochs in which social structures meet the needs of the roles they produce and maintain, little change in roles will occur. Indeed, attempts to remold roles will be constrained. When structure and roles do not mesh, however, roles will be altered in an attempt to adjust to the structural changes [Stryker, 1987:93]. When the "one drop rule" prevailed throughout our society, the racial structure, as displayed on the Census, job applications, and SAT forms, did not encourage role improvisation. Most Americans did not imagine a need for multiracial categories on forms. Large numbers of black-white Americans did not claim to be both black and white. Today, however, this same racial structure does not meet the needs of the increasing numbers of biracial Americans who wish to acknowledge publicly both sides of their racial identity. The transformation in racial identity is now challenging the traditional racial role of black-white Americans and the social structure that tells them to choose between races.

According to Sheldon Stryker, race is a "master status" because it is a "structurally-based attribute that (a) derive[s] from pervasive features of the social structure, particularly stratification features, in which role relationships are embedded; (b) do[es] not in [itself] provide the grounds for specific networks of social interaction; but (c) enter[s] the formation and interactional content of many of the specific networks of interaction in which persons play a role." He maintains that "a master status is perhaps as much or more defined by the responses of others not incorporated into our interactional networks as by those who are or as by our own 'identification with' processes" [Stryker, 1987:100,101].

Interestingly, the transformation of racial identity process itself therefore calls into question the definition of race as a "master status." As described in Chapter 3, the racial definition of biracial Americans is now most keenly influenced by those with whom they interact, rather than by the traditional racial structure. No longer is black racial heritage an irrevocable "master status" for biracial Americans.

SOCIOLOGY, RACE, AND THE TRANSFORMATION

Despite the reference to race as a social construction, not one of the above theorists appears to have considered possible the transformation of racial identity among individuals or a group of individuals. Today, however, many of what were once considered "master statuses" are now much more fluid. The much ballyhooed mutability of both sex and gender are prime examples. The idea of race as a permeable concept is found often in popular literature. In February 1995, *Newsweek* devoted an entire issue to the question "What is black?" Noting both the superficial biological differences between the traditionally demarcated races and the increasing numbers of multiracial immigrants and American citizens, *Newsweek* declared that "the markers of racial identity are every conceivable hue—and suddenly ideology and attitude matter as much as pigmentation" [Morganthau, 2/23/95:63–65].

Reflecting the idea that race is simply a matter of ideology is the growing trend of American teenagers to simply choose a race. An article by Nell Bernstein in *West* magazine, the Sunday supplement to the *San José Mercury News* [Bernstein,11/13/94:87–90] describes how teenagers in a California suburb "claim" various racial identities. White girls declare themselves Mexican, while some Mexican boys assert they are descendants of white neighborhood toughs. As one young Californian observes, "The boys all wanna be black, the girls all wanna be Mexican. It's the glamour."[6] Some teenagers today feel they can simply choose to identify racially with any group they admire. As racial minorities in California become the majority, many young Americans believe it is now hip to be nonwhite. For many teenagers, having two white parents is no obstacle to their desire to be Mexican or black.

As the United States becomes increasingly diverse, it is necessary for sociologists to acknowledge that race is no longer necessarily a master status. While the example of white teenagers becoming black described by Bernstein is an extreme representation of this change in the status of race, it is nonetheless one that is indicative of current changes in the racial structure of the United States. The current Census categories of White, Black (Not Hispanic), Hispanic, Asian or

Pacific Islander, American Indian, Eskimo, Aleut, or Other are simply no longer adequate. In the 1990 U.S. Census, by using a write-in blank form, "Americans claimed membership in nearly 300 races or ethnic groups and 600 American Indian Tribes. Hispanics had 70 categories of their own" [Morganthau, 2/13/95:67–69]. The social psychologist Kay Deaux reports that her own data has revealed ethnic groups claim[ing] a previously unclaimed ethnic identity or . . . deny[ing] one that was formerly salient" [Deaux, 1992:27].

Clearly, there is now a power struggle going on in the attempts to change the present racial structure in the United States. Those who have benefited from the traditional racial structure and wish to maintain their advantage now battle the cultural and historical forces described in Chapter 3, as well as those multiracial persons who will profit from a more open racial structure. Ironically, many traditionally oppressed racial groups also resist the current and proposed changes in racial demarcation, fearing the softening of racial boundaries will lead to the loss of recently achieved rights and programs of accessibility. Multiracial Americans who wish to acknowledge publicly all sides of their racial heritage must deal with these two groups of persons in their struggle for multiracial boxes on racial classification forms. Meanwhile, all three groups face the growing cry of those persons who favor the abolition of all types of racial classifications.

"The tactics of appropriation and processes of identification that are involved in articulating identity and compelling recognition always invoke and transform fields of power" [Coombe, 1993:412]. Various interests that struggle for power in society compete in the quest to control identity formation. These power plays should be the focus of sociological analysis. The symbolic interactionist perspective illuminates this struggle. Using Stryker, in conjunction with Glaser and Strauss and McCall and Simmons, is useful in this endeavor.

Glaser and Strauss aid us in defining the transformation of racial identity as a status passage. Their work enables us to identify it and prepare for attempts at reversing the process by those who find the passage to be undesirable. McCall and Simmons warn us of the necessity of having a clearly discernible identity in our impersonal society. They also teach us of the roles of the family, or "gatekeeper," and the larger society in influencing the hierarchy of each person's identity set. Finally, Stryker aids us in our understanding of how structure affects identity formation and transformation. He apprises us of how the structural aspects of society constrain our identity choices. When the structural aspects of society change, so do the constraints on individual persons.

While abstruse to different degrees, all of the above theories can be directly and clearly applied to the transformation of racial identity among biracial Americans. The transformation is a "rite of passage." The racial role-identities of black-white Americans are being transformed due, in large part, to the changing constraints of society etched out in identity theory. The historical changes in U.S. culture and law in the last thirty years have prompted a loosening of constraints on the attributions and choices of racial definition for biracial Americans. No longer are they successfully compelled by the prevailing social structure to identify as black and black alone. Race, like gender,[7] is a product of our culture.

There is no guarantee, however, that the transformation in racial identity will lead to continued and increasing choice of racial identity among Americans. A backlash, such as the one that occurred at the end of post-Civil War Reconstruction, could ensue. An economic depression or other societal crisis could result in greater friction and subsequent distinction between races. Americans may once again feel forced to choose to live on only one side of the color line.

Today forces on both sides of the transformation process are at work. There are those who desire to halt the passage from black to biracial and there are those who wish to charter the passage. As culture changes, so do our definitions of "What is black?" and now "What is biracial?" These are postmodern questions. We now turn to the postmodern answers to these queries.

POSTMODERNISM AND THE TRANSFORMATION

As identities become increasingly relative, symbolic interactionists would do well to incorporate some of the postmodern perspective. Indeed, important aspects of current postmodernism were foreseen and discussed by early symbolic interactionist theorists. The postmodern focus on the symbolic was one of the primary focuses of the founders of symbolic interactionism. Georg Simmel, one of the founding theorists of symbolic interactionism, anticipated many thoughts now trumpeted by postmodern sociologists. In *The Web of Group Affiliations* [1955] he discusses the concept of overlapping identities. These ideas are newly packaged by such postmodern theorists as Kenneth Gergen, who writes of the "saturated self" [1991].

Symbolic interactionists and postmodern theorists both maintain that the "self-identity" is "socially constructed, emergent, and plural" [Shalim, 1993:304]. However, as identity theorists grapple with such mundane questions as "Why is it that one person, given a free weekend afternoon, chooses to take his or her children to the zoo while another person opts to spend that time on the golf course with friends?" [Stryker, *Encyclopedia of Sociology*, 1992:871], they are ceding the field of transformation of identity to postmodernists. In doing so, they leave the examination of the transformation in the hands of persons who view the subject from an alternate point of view. While both symbolic interactionists and postmodern theorists agree that identity is socially constructed, their conceptions of society and their level of analysis differ tremendously.

Postmodern theorists approach the issue of identity from a distinct perspective. Unlike symbolic interactionists, the postmodern approach is on a social-structural plane. They eschew examinations of individuals and small communities. Postmodern concepts are large in scope. They analyze the concept of identity from a societal, rather than a personal, level.

There are no true identities for postmodern theorists. Postmodernists, such as Jean Baudrillard and Jean-Françoise Lyotard, believe that the self identities of persons have been destroyed by "the bombardment of fragmented signs and images which erode all sense of continuity between past, present, and future, all teleological belief that life is a meaningful project." Life is merely a conglomeration of scattered and disconnected "experiences and images" [Feathersone, 1995:44]. Stable identities are no longer possible. To Baudrillard and Lyotard, the questions "What is black?" and "What is race?" are simply examples of the impossibility of real identities. There is no sure grounding for any type of identity—racial or nonracial.

Such fundamental concepts as class and class conflict have "imploded" according to Baudrillard [1983]. The division between the simulated and the real no longer exists. Facsimiles now govern society, which has become a "hyperreality." Image and reality can no longer be distinguished. Lyotard, like Baudrillard, dismisses all attempts at universal understanding. He maintains that the world has become "fragmented." According to Lyotard, consensus results in false reasoning [1984]. In fact, Lyotard goes so far as to say that such attempts at universalities are "terrororistic" policies [Kellner, 1990:271]. Given that they believe there is no reality, even for individual self-concepts, postmodern theorists would clearly argue against any definitive attempt to conceptualize racial identity.

Both Baudrillard and Lyotard espouse no faith in the potential for political or other forms of large-scale societal progress. Neither believes persons capable of agency. Like other postmodern theorists, they maintain that "the autonomous, self-constituting subject that was the achievement of modern individuals, of a culture of individualism, is fragmenting and disappearing, owing to the social processes and the leveling of individuality in a rationalized, bureaucratized, mediatized, and consumerized mass society" [Kellner, 1992:143]. Persons possess neither the capability of maintaining a firm identity nor undertaking a transformation of that identity. There are no true answers for postmodern theorists; reality is fiction. These theorists maintain that where one is "situated" in the world is the key to identity analysis. Identity, as well as everything else, is relative. Persons must merely reflect the images of themselves assigned to them by the prevailing simulacra in society—which has no basis in reality.

Postmodern theorists expose the fluid nature of reality. However, while showing that identity is closely tied to social structure and history, they lose sight of the power of persons to shape their own identity. Earlier chapters have shown, while biracial identity is inherently tied up with the history of black/white relations in the United States, individual Americans can respond to that history and transform identity(ies).

The fault of postmodern theorists lies at the other end of the spectrum from that of symbolic interactionists. While symbolic interactionist do not adequately acknowledge the current breadth and depth of fluidity of identities, postmodernists are unable to grasp the persistent tangibility of identities. For a postmodernist, a transformation of identity is merely a change in image. The former identity did not really exist, and the transformed image of identity is no more real than the former identity. Moreover, the possiblity of persons successfully finding and then transforming their identities does not exist. But identities do exist—and they can be transformed—thus the need for a new theory of identity that incorporates the most useful elements of symbolic interactionism and postmodernism.

A THEORY OF IDENTITY FOR TODAY

I maintain that while there is a paradigm shift in identities today, self-identities are not becoming relativized into nonexistence. The shift is a powerful and disruptive one, however. The binary description of attributes as ascribed (e.g., sex, gender, race) and achieved (e.g., income, marital status, educational level) is no longer applicable in today's world. We must now add a tertiary group of attributes—those that are chosen.[8] This third group has effectively challenged those attributes that were once confidently deemed ascribed or "master statuses."

For all of us, knowing who we are is increasingly complicated. Boundaries are blurring. The questionable race of a biracial person is simply one example. Other identities that were once firm are now in flux. Gender and sex roles are no longer clear. Gender-bending[9] on the Internet, sex-change operations, the increasing acceptability of bisexuals, and stay-at-home fathers and work-obsessed mothers are some instances of the current permeability of once seemingly ascribed attributes.

It is important to acknowledge, however, that while identities have become more fluid, their roles in each person's life and society in general are still firm. The biracial persons interviewed who do not wish to identify themselves racially, nonetheless, have clear identities. Other aspects of their identities are simply more salient. Likewise, those who maintain identities as both black and white are not necessarily confused as to who they are. They merely have a more complex understanding of their racial identity than society would normally allow a generation ago. Similarly, monoracial persons who are juggling many role-identities in their lives (e.g., father, mayor, husband, basketball player) still maintain a lucid sense of themselves.

The dialectic between society and identity continues. As society becomes globalized and the economy shifts, persons' identities adjust by becoming more fluid. As identities change, so do persons' demands on society. This in turn prompts a further alteration in the social structure. This has implications on all levels of society. For instance, as more mothers, spurred on by decreasing family incomes, join the workforce, the demand for adequate day care, family leave-time, and after-school programs becomes more urgent. All these needs are now being discussed at the highest political levels in the United States.

Identity politics is alive and well in the United States. In a nation where political power is based on either organized money or organized people, those persons with a collective self-interest who band together can affect the social structure. The Family Leave Act was signed by President Clinton in 1993. Likewise, as increasing numbers of interracial parents and their offspring advocate a multiracial category on racial classification forms, members of the Bureau of the

Census take note. There is a strong possibility that a multiracial box will be added to the Census 2000. The social, political, and economic ramifications of such a change, which will be discussed in Chapter 7, are enormous.

Clearly, the transformation of racial identity has a strong impact on society. Neither the symbolic interactionist nor the postmodern perspective is adequately equipped to address the ramifications of the transformation. They do offer a starting point, however.

While symbolic interactionists have not addressed the increasing fluidity of the most basic identities, they provide a solid grounding for understanding identity development and transformation. Postmodernists, on the other hand, allow us the freedom to acknowledge that all identities are open to challenge. Between these two perspectives lies a vision that enables us to comprehend and analyze the current flux of identities in our society. As society transforms and becomes more fluid, so do our identities. But just as the world around us still exists, so do our transformed identities. Although they may be more complex than in the past, they are still, nonetheless, real. It is the tangible actions of persons who maintain these identities that will produce the next transformation in identities. Chapter 7 examines the public policy ramifications of the current transformation in racial identity among biracial persons.

NOTES

1. Twelve original and two additional properties of status passages were laid out by Glaser and Strauss, *Status Passages*, 1971:4–5.

2. This includes persons trying to stop their own passage and those who wish to stop the passage of one or more other persons.

3. In 1995, the Bureau of Labor Statistics conducted a survey of 60,000 households that revealed that when a multiracial category was made available, "there was no statistically significant decline in the number of Americans identifying themselves as blacks, whites, or Asians." The sole group that had reduced numbers with the multiracial category was Native Americans [Mathews, 7/6/96,:p. A1, col.1.].

4. Just as my analysis of black-white biracial identity is a product of 1990s American society.

5. Those behaviors typically performed by an individual in a particular situation.

6. I assume "glamour" refers to being a member of a popular and, perhaps, exotic ethnic/racial group.

7. See Judith Lorber's *Paradoxes of Gender* [1994] for an in-depth analysis of gender as a construct of the development of human culture.

8. While there has always been some degree of choice in whom one could be, the relative influence of constraints on such choices has changed dramatically. For instance, one hundred years ago, a person perceived as black could maintain a biracial identity. However, the personal cost, and lack of societal support, for such an identity would have been tremendous. The constraints against a black-white American choosing to maintain a biracial identity today are much less than they were a century ago.

9. Posing as one gender and living as another.

7

Public Policy Implications

The increasing fluidity of racial identities in the United States has clear public policy implications. Questions about race define who faces discrimination and who benefits from social and economic programs designed to prevent and compensate for past and present racial discrimination. These uncertainties have stoked the fire of the current debate over a potential multiracial category in the Census 2000. This chapter focuses on all three of these issues—discrimination, affirmative action, and the Census 2000—as they apply to biracial Americans.

DISCRIMINATION

Racial discrimination still abounds in the United States. Although Civil Rights legislation has made direct discrimination illegal, it nevertheless occurs throughout the nation. One of the areas in which racial discrimination is most common is the marketplace. In every aspect of the retail economy, Americans with dark skin face negative attitudes and actions that white-appearing persons never encounter. From the extra scrutiny of security persons, to the rudeness of store attendants, to employment discrimination, black men and women must run a gauntlet when they participate in the American marketplace. Even traveling to the store to face such treatment can be a difficult endeavor for African Americans or mixed-race persons who appear black. Poor Americans of color may find there is no accessible public transportation, while those minorities who can afford a taxi may find that none will respond to their hails.

Widespread segregation persists between white and black Americans [Marger, 1994:268]. Lower-class African Americans, usually in inner-city ghettos, are especially isolated from white America [Goldsmith and Blakely, 1992]. One typical means of separating poor urban African Americans from middle- and upper-class white persons is geographical segregation. As cities become predominantly minority, white suburbanites strive to prevent poor urban residents from leaving the inner city. This enforced separation is also evident in the marketplace. Municipal bus lines rarely travel to suburban shopping centers, making it difficult for poor inner-city residents to do their shopping out of the city. This relates to what social scientists now refer to as "social triage" [Derber, 1996]: the isolation of poor, minority, inner-city communities from the rest of society.

As noted earlier, middle-class and wealthy persons who appear black may also face racial discrimination with regard to transportation. For example, in the preface to *Race Matters* [1993], the eminent theologian and philosopher Cornel West discusses one of his encounters with racism as taxi after taxi refused to stop for him in New York City. Immaculately dressed as usual, West was on his way to meet a photographer to shoot the cover for his new book.

I waited and waited and waited. After the ninth taxi refused me my blood began to boil. The tenth taxi refused me and stopped for a kind, well-dressed, smiling female fellow citizen of European descent. As she stepped in the cab, she said, "This is really ridiculous, is it not?"

Ugly racial memories of the past flashed through my mind. Years ago, while driving from New York to teach at Williams College, I was stopped on fake charges of trafficking cocaine. When I told the police officer I was a professor of religion, he replied, "Yeh, and I'm the Flying Nun. Let's go, nigger!" I was stopped three times in my first ten days in Princeton for driving too slowly on a residential street with a speed limit of twenty-five miles per hour (And my son, Clifton, already has similar memories at the tender age of fifteen). [1993:xv]

While the white woman who took the cab commented that the situation was "ridiculous," she also did not hesitate to take West's cab. This is symbolic of a "realpolitik" liberal's view of racial discrimination: "It's a pity and something really should be done about it, but I'm not willing to compromise my own position or advantage."

There is also abundant evidence that racial discrimination still exists in the hiring and promotion process. Some employers make efforts to direct racial minorities to backroom, dead-end positions. For example, in 1993, evidence was found that 211 officials of the Shoney's restaurant chain used discriminatory tactics in their hiring techniques. Applications were marked to specify the race of the prospective employee. Those black persons who were hired were assigned to the kitchen area "so that all employees in the dining area would be white" [Bergmann, 1996:49].

Also in 1993, researchers at the Urban Institute discovered that among young men with identical experience, manners, and dress, the "white men were offered jobs 45 percent more often than the young black men" [Bergmann, 1996:51]. Research such as this makes it possible to understand the disparities between numbers of white and black workers at such companies as NYNEX. As of 1992, African Americans comprised only 1.7 percent of the NYNEX workforce in the greater Boston area. Considering that 7.3 percent of the general population in this area is black, racial discrimination seems obvious. In one NYNEX branch in the area, not one of its 116 employees was black [Bergmann, 1996:58].

In November 1996, Texaco was forced to settle a race bias suit for $176 million, the largest settlement of its kind ever. Texaco executives were caught on tape making derogatory comments about blacks while planning to destroy evidence that could be used against them in the racial discrimination suit. When the tapes were made public, a coalition of anti-racism groups established a nationwide boycott against Texaco. At that point, Texaco's CEO, Peter Bijur, fired the executives involved and made a public apology, forcefully denouncing racism and pledging to root it out of Texaco. If his intentions are true, Bijur has much work to do. A good place for him to start might be at the top. Of the 873 executives at Texaco "earning more than $106,000, only six are black" [Cockburn, 1996].

NYNEX, Shoney's, and Texaco are not alone. According to a 1990 *National Law Journal* poll concerning discrimination in the workplace, 48 percent of whites and 64 percent of blacks questioned maintained that every, or almost every, employer practices discrimination "regardless of their official policies" [Steinberg, 1995:153]. Clearly, racial discrimination is alive and well.

One device created to offset past and present racial discrimination is affirmative action (AA). Today just the mention of the two words "affirmative" and "action" sets off a cacophony of opinions for and against the concept and actual AA programs.[1] As the debate over race-based preferences rises in volume, it is increasingly unclear to many just what the term "affirmative action" signifies.

AFFIRMATIVE ACTION

In 1964, Congress passed a Civil Rights Act. It granted, for the first time in U.S. history, equal rights to racial minorities. Title VII of the Civil Rights Act created the Equal Employment Opportunities Commission (EEOC) and prohibited discrimination in the workplace on the basis of race, sex, national origin, and religion. President Lyndon B. Johnson had a further vision, however. In his June 4, 1965 speech at Howard University, he stated that equal opportunity was not sufficient. "You do not take a person who, for years, has been hobbled by chains and liberate him, bring him up to the starting line of a race and then say, 'you are free to compete with all the others,' and still justly believe that you have been completely fair. . . . We seek not just freedom but opportunity—not just legal equity but human ability—not just equality as a right and a theory but equality as a fact and as a result" [quote found in Rainwater and Yancey, 1967:125–32]. This idea of "equality as a fact and as a result" led the way to the creation of affirmative action programs designed to ensure such equality between the races. Later in 1965, President Johnson, by executive order, required federal contractors to establish goals and timetables to ensure equitable minority group representation in their companies.

In the following decade, affirmative action programs became more widespread. In 1972, the Equal Opportunity Act directed most federal contractors and subcontractors, all state governments and institutions, and most local governments to increase the percentage of their minority employees to match the proportion of minorities in the pool of prospective employees. Two years later, in 1974, President Nixon ordered compliance reviews to ensure follow-through with the program. Those found in noncompliance were required to meet government-initiated goals and timetables.

While all large organizations associated in any way with the federal government (e.g., colleges accepting federal scholarship money or loans) must establish affirmative action programs, private companies that have fifty or fewer people on payroll are exempt from such regulations. According to the U.S. Census, approximately one-third of all employees in the United States work in such small companies. Therefore, a major portion of the American workforce exists outside the realm of affirmative action.

While the examples of present-day discrimination make it clear that affirmative action is not a panacea for discrimination, there are many Americans who believe it is a positive step against racial bias. On the other hand, growing numbers of citizens decry affirmative action and favor its abolishment. There are also large numbers of persons who approve of the concept of affirmative action but disapprove of how it is carried out. For instance, surveys of both California and Massachusetts citizens show support for affirmative action in theory but not in practice. While almost half of Californians favor affirmative action, two-thirds oppose "granting preferential treatment to" anyone in public employment, education or contracting" by a margin of two to one [Pertman, 10/5/96:A1]. Massachusetts residents concur. They "overwhelmingly support affirmative action in theory, but when presented with many of its everyday applications—government setasides, hiring preferences and race-based scholarships—the support dissolves into opposition" [McGrory, 5/21/95:A31].

The Case against Affirmative Action

Many of those who oppose affirmative action maintain that it is actually "reverse discrimination." In their eyes, AA "is now a widely accepted euphemism for institutionalized favoritism" [Cohen, 1995:3]. In *The New Color Line*, Craig Roberts and Lawrence Stratton aptly sum up the argument for many, stating that President Johnson went too far when he proposed equality of result rather than mere equality of opportunity.

In place of equality under the law and a color-blind society in which people are judged by their merit, we are confronted with the rise of new preferment based on race and gender. A new status-based legal system is evolving that allocates jobs, promotions, university admissions, board memberships, bonuses and awards, mortgage financing, voting outcomes, university tenure, access to training programs and gifted programs, and even reprimands and disciplinary action proportionately by race and gender. [1995:127]

When Roberts, Stratton, and their allies look at affirmative action, they see a system of racial and gender preference with no regard to individual rights. The good and acceptable idea to ensure equal treatment has "been turned completely on its head. What was once the name for the active pursuit of equal treatment regardless of race has become the name for instruments designed to give deliberate preference on the basis of race" [Cohen, 1995:4].

These men and women believe it is a terrible mistake to repeat in reverse the error of past racial discrimination. Carl Cohen, the author of *Naked Racial Preference* denounces affirmative action, writing, "The sorry history of discrimination against blacks in this country no one will deny. But now to repeat that story with a different set of victims—once again burdened by color of skin!—is irony almost too bitter to swallow" [1995:216].

Some beneficiaries of affirmative action also oppose AA programs. Agreeing with white male opponents of AA, many conservative black leaders lament the derogatory effects of being "affirmative action babies" [Carter, 1991]. Sparked by Thomas Sowell's [1976] anti-affirmative action work, such African American luminaries as Stephen Carter, Shelby Steele, and Clarence Thomas have joined the chorus of successful black men who say "no thanks" to preferential treatment. They each speak of the taint of inferiority affirmative action has left upon them. They lament that others perceive them as quota fillers rather than deserving and qualified applicants for the positions they fill.

The word "quota" has become the mudslinging term that "liberal" began to be during the Bush-Dukakis presidential election. Many people who oppose affirmative action believe such programs are now simply a system of rigidly enforced goals and timetables. While they may approve of the aspect of AA that requires institutions actively to encourage applications from qualified minorities, they disapprove of any directives to attain a specific number of minority admittees or employees. In many persons' eyes, these quotas are now synonymous with affirmative action. Declaring their innocence from any sort of racism, these men and women decry affirmative action quotas as an evil set against the Civil Rights gains fought for so valiantly in the 1950s and 1960s.

The Case for Affirmative Action

While many proponents of affirmative action deny that these programs are based on quotas, clearly, goals and timetables are an integral part of any effective program designed to ensure racial equality in employment or admissions. In *In Defense of Affirmative Action* [1996], Barbara Bergmann, asserts that quotas are a necessary aspect of affirmative action: "The cause of honest debate over the costs and benefits of affirmative action is probably served if those defending affirmative action acknowledge that such programs do have quotalike aspects." These quotas are needed because most employers would not otherwise make "good faith" efforts to achieve racial parity in the workplace [Bergmann, 1996:13].

There is evidence that "good faith" efforts are not enough. It is difficult to believe that certain companies compelled to maintain affirmative action programs will do so when AA no longer exists. Today, even with affirmative action policies in place, many companies are not accountable. For instance, the Ford Motor Company conducts business with the U.S. government, "yet in 1992 only 4 percent of its managerial jobs were occupied by women; at many other large companies, 30 to 50 percent of managers performing similar functions were women" [Bergmann, 1996:8]. Obviously affirmative action has not been effectively enforced at Ford.

But the U.S. government has rarely enforced Civil Rights laws thoroughly and effectively. The latest report from the Commission on Civil Rights [June 1995] revealed that "funding and staffing provided for civil rights enforcement have diminished over the last 15 years. . . . Although resources have increased since FY [fiscal year] 1989, the enforcement responsibilities of these agencies have also grown enormously, and the reductions in funding and staff continue to undermine our national enforcement of civil rights" [p. 4]. This indicates that affirmative action policies have lacked enforcement at more than just the Ford Motor Company.

The U.S. Senate itself is still a bastion of white male superiority. As of 1996, the Senate was 92 percent male and 97 percent white. White males have always held the presidency. American women and racial minorities are still not represented in proportion to their numbers. These statistics are fuel for the argument to maintain AA.

Advocates of affirmative action scoff at the now popular notion that the United States no longer needs race-based preferential programs. Stephen Steinberg, in *Turning Back*, delivers a caustic argument against those who would dissolve affirmative action programs. He maintains that equality in the workplace is doomed without enforced quotas. Like Bergmann, Steinberg reminds us that

what Justice Thomas and most opponents of affirmative action forget is that good-faith efforts to increase minority representation were generally ineffective until they were backed up by specific "goals and timetables" that, in effect, gave preference to minority applicants who met basic qualifications but might not have been hired or promoted without affirmative action mandates. [1995:165,166]

The Future of Affirmative Action

The constitutionality of affirmative action programs has been hotly debated. The Supreme Court itself has wavered on the issue. For example, in 1978, the Court ruled racial quotas unconstitutional (*University of California v. Bakke*), but the very next year it upheld them in a private business and union agreement (*United Steelworkers of America v. Weber*).

More recently an increasingly conservative court has sharply curbed affirmative action. On June 12, 1995, Justice O'Connor, speaking for the majority, ruled in the case of *Adaraand Constructors, Inc. v. Peña, Secretary of*

Transportation that "any person, of whatever race, has the right to demand that any governmental actor, subject to the Constitution, justify any racial classification subjecting that person to unequal treatment under the strictest judicial scrutiny" [quote found in Cohen, 1995:236]. In a decision that split the court five to four, the justices declared that government affirmative action programs must "be based only in the government's 'compelling interest,' subject to 'strict scrutiny' for constitutionality, and that they be 'narrowly tailored' to remedy the effects of specifically documented discrimination" [Bergmann, 1996:92].

The Court ruled in the *Adaraand* case that it is unconstitutional for the federal government to award bonuses to institutions that hire minority contractors at the expense of white contractors. Such a practice is a violation of the Fourteenth Amendment to the constitution, which ensures equal rights for all citizens. Preferential treatment for minorities can occur only on occasions when discrimination has been proven and the preferential actions will specifically remedy that case of discrimination. Affirmative action will now be subject to scrutiny on a case-by-case basis. In each case, discrimination must be verified and preferential treatment for minorities deemed necessary to alleviate that particular incident of discrimination.

For instance, a minority contractor seeking preferential consideration from the federal government must prove both that the government practiced discriminatory hiring practices and that special treatment for him or her will correct the proven instance of discrimination. In this manner, white contractors, as a group, will not be unduly punished for instances of discrimination in which they, as individuals, played no part. They will have to resign themselves to minority contractors receiving preference over them only in the confirmed instances of discrimination that can be clearly rectified through the hiring of a minority contractor. In cases where discrimination cannot be proven, and then perceived to be solvable through preferential treatment of minorities, affirmative action is deemed unconstitutional.

Affirmative action has also come under attack outside the judicial system, with the state of California at the forefront of the battle. The vote in California provides "a preview of the national debate" [Pertman, 10/5/96:A1]. The first major defeat for AA in that state arrived on July 20, 1995 when the regents of the nine campuses of the University of California voted to end affirmative action systemwide. On November 5, 1996, residents of California passed Proposition 209, an initiative that bans affirmative action in the state. Passionate and intemperate outbursts have arisen from both advocates and opponents of the proposition. Riot police were called out to ensure order at the California State University when David Duke, the former Ku Klux Klan leader, came to support the proposition in a debate at the Northridge campus.

However, at the same time affirmative action is being threatened by both judges and lawmakers, it has found an ally in the business world. During the Reagan and Bush administrations, when affirmative action was under concerted attack, the Equal Opportunity Advisory Council (comprised of more than 270 companies) and the National Association of Manufacturers effectively "quashed" every effort to dismantle affirmative action requirements for companies that conduct business with the federal government [Bergmann, 1996:160]. Corporate leaders are very aware that affirmative action is good for the long-term health of the U.S. economy. Census figures indicate that white men comprised only 41 percent of the American workforce in 1994. The number is expected to continue to decrease.

Business persons realize that the pool of potential and qualified employees will become dangerously low unless racial minorities and women are added to the mix in substantial numbers. It appears likely that, even if affirmative action is stripped of any legal backing, smart corporations will continue some form of AA on a voluntary basis. Although the government will no longer grant bonuses to certain institutions that give preference to minorities, an informal version of affirmative action will continue even after official affirmative action policies are dismantled. Employers, taking care to avoid lawsuits by hiring only qualified minority candidates, will most likely continue the practice of affirmative action successfully until persons of color are more proportionally represented in the business sector.

Aside from merely avoiding poor public relations that come with a racist and sexist reputation, there are other profit-driven reasons for corporations to enact a version of affirmative action. A company must understand the commercial needs and desires of potential consumers of their goods. As U.S. companies with predominantly white leadership strive to succeed in both a multiracial American and a global market, it makes sense for them to hire a capable minority, rather than a white male, who is, perhaps, even more qualified for the position. It is good business for a company to make sure its staff knows what the public wants. In a nation whose population is increasingly racially diverse, a firm whose employees resemble that diversity has an edge over businesses with a primarily white workforce.

Another question of concern for the affirmative action debate is the increasing numbers of biracial and multiracial Americans. With more and more Americans of mixed race, the obvious question that comes to mind is "Who qualifies for affirmative action?" Just how much black, Hispanic, Native American, etc. ancestry must one have to benefit from affirmative action? The raw truth is that affirmative action is now benefiting persons whom AA lawmakers never considered. Affirmative action was devised before the biracial baby boom began in 1967. Should these biracial baby boomers qualify for affirmative action?

Today, whether they appear black, mixed racial, or white, biracial persons do qualify for affirmative action. All persons who declare themselves to be a racial minority are eligible for preferential consideration. Under affirmative action, both corporations and certain individuals benefit from ambiguous racial designations. Companies meet their quotas more easily when persons with mixed race backgrounds qualify for affirmative action. There is a danger, however, that mixed racial Americans may be the first to fill positions set aside for monoracial minorities. Because they may appear "whiter," biracial employees may be more palatable for an employer under pressure to hire racial minorities.

Moreover, because the majority of biracial persons come from the middle and professional classes, the advantages they gain from AA work to separate further middle- and upper-middle class African Americans who qualify for positions affected by these programs and poor blacks without the education necessary for such jobs. Light-complected blacks dominate the middle and professional classes of African Americans. Evidence indicates that "dark-skinned blacks suffer much the same disadvantages relative to light-skinned blacks that blacks, in general, suffer relative to whites [Hughes and Hertel, 1990:1112]. Increased numbers of biracial Americans benefiting from AA only exacerbates this trend. These dilemmas illustrate how the present monoracial structure simply no longer works in an increasingly multiracial society. In turn, our increasing multiracial population calls affirmative action, in its present form, into question.

Debate now also swarms around the categorization of racial groups in the United States. The Office of Management and Budget's (OMB) *Statistical Policy Directive No. 15*, adopted in 1977, provides the following racial and ethnic categories for such federal programs as affirmative action and general federal statistics: (a) American Indian or Alaskan Native (b) Asian or Pacific Islander (c) Black (Not Hispanic) (d) Hispanic (e) White. Many Americans advocate a revision of this directive that would allow for accurate racial categorization of biracial and multiracial Americans.[2]

MULTIRACIAL CATEGORIES

As discussed in Chapter 6, a movement to add a multiracial category to the Census 2000 now exists.[3] A change in Directive 15 would allow an alteration in the Census racial categorizations. Project RACE (Reclassify All Children Equally) is one of the major groups leading the struggle for a change in racial designations.

Project RACE advocates official recognition of multiracial persons through legal and legislative channels. The implications of such a category extend well beyond the political realm. For example, the lack of consideration of multiracial persons in reference to prescriptive drug use is one issue of particular concern for them. For instance, one pharmaceutical company created a drug to fight hypertension. They recommended that white persons take one milligram and black persons consume two milligrams per dosage. When questioned what size dosage multiracial persons should consume, the company admitted they had no idea. No multiracial persons were included in the clinical trials of the drug, emphasizing the fact that recognition of such a category is important not only for the psychological and social well-being of this population, but also for their physical health. Project RACE campaigns for full use of multiracial persons in tests of new drugs.

Susan Graham, the executive director of Project RACE and herself a white mother of a biracial child, maintains that mixed racial persons should have the same right as monoracial persons to define themselves accurately on racial classification forms [Matthews, 8/6/96:A1]. She advocates the creation of a multiracial category with subheadings consisting of all designated races. Respondents with a variety of racial heritages would check off multiracial and then check off as many racial subcategories as apply. This method of racial demarcation allows mixed racial persons to have a universal racial label—multiracial—while recognizing their unique racial backgrounds.[4]

The ability to affirm all aspects of their racial identity is important to many multiracial persons. Lise Funderburg maintains that multiracial persons should be able to check any and all boxes that apply. Minority groups would not lose numerical representation in this manner. For instance, all those with African heritage would fill out African on their Census form, as well as any other applicable race(s). As Funderburg admits, however, this system would be much more complicated than either the present Census form or one proposed version that would include a single multiracial category. However, as she sagely points out, "increasingly, the United States is made up of a more complicated population" [Funderburg, 7/10/96:A15]. Project RACE's suggestion that includes both a multiracial category as well as specific racial groups seems the appropriate solution. It is time for the Census to mirror truly the population it attempts to measure—complications and all.[5]

Organization in the movement for a multiracial category still needs fine-tuning, however. A July rally intended to draw "thousands" on the Mall in Washington "to celebrate multiracial identity and to add a multiracial category to the next census" attracted headlines but only netted a mere two hundred persons on the Mall [New York Times, 7/20/96:A1 and Boston Globe, 7/21/96:A21]. It appears that this was the result of a lack of real organization behind the event. In March, Charles Michael Byrd, the publisher of "Interracial Voice" on the Internet and cited as the rally organizer by the Boston Globe, reported that there was not then a huge response for the march. It is difficult to understand, therefore, why news sources such as the New York Times and the Boston Globe were told to expect "thousands" at the rally. It appears the organizers breached a basic rule of grassroots organizing: always know the level of your support.

One reason the multiracial rally in Washington turned out such a sparse crowd was the paucity of multiracial persons aware of its occurrence. Astonishingly, Byrd confined his organizing efforts to the Internet and press releases that did not include a phone number for those seeking information about the rally.[6] No interviewee brought up the topic, and not one of the six interviewees directly questioned about the rally had heard of it. Significantly, each indicated they were happy to know of the event but frustrated they were not recruited and informed in time to attend the rally.

Despite disorganization among some factions of the multiracial movement, the establishment of a multiracial category seems both sensible and inescapable. Our present monoracial classification form no longer suffices in our increasingly biracial and multiracial society. The time has come to change the racial classification system to reflect the U.S. population more accurately.

The revision of Directive 15 and the Census categories would have a profound impact on the social well-being of many biracial and multiracial Americans. The official racial recognition of this population will give them a validated and unifying term of identification. It will also ensure their inclusion in future drug testing and other areas of health concern.

The inevitable reformation of the racial classification system loses some significance as federally regulated affirmative action withers under constitutional and electoral challenges to its legitimacy. Informal, business- initiated affirmative action will soon be the norm. Just as racial appearance now largely determines the extent to which biracial persons face race-based discrimination, it will soon designate who benefits from unofficial affirmative action programs.

If businesses, no longer under obligation to use monoracially-based classification forms to ensure racial parity, still desire their workforce to mirror society, they will use racial appearance as their guidepost. With the elimination of official affirmative action racial classification forms, racial appearance, rather than official racial identity, will then determine who benefits from unofficial affirmative action efforts. The importance of race will not evaporate, but its means of determination will change to match our post-affirmative action, increasingly diverse society.

But how do biracial individuals themselves feel about these complex issues? Now that we have explored some of the political and structural implications of the increasing numbers of multiracial Americans and the transformation of racial identity among biracial persons, I will close with their perspectives. Biracial persons view the changing racial demographics in the United States from a unique vantage point. They experience both the hardships of historic racial discrimination and the possibilities of racial harmony. What follows are their perceptions and stories of discrimination, affirmative action, and multiracial categories.

BIRACIAL PERSONS AND DISCRIMINATION

As described in examples throughout the preceding chapters, biracial persons must continually confront racial discrimination. Personal tales of these discriminatory acts abound. Discrimination in the marketplace was noted earlier in this chapter. There, too, many biracial persons face the same racially-based injustices as do black Americans. Several male interviewees, who appear African American, discussed experiences when security guards followed them in stores. As men perceived as black in a white-dominated racist society, they are used to such discrimination. As noted in Chapter 2, when a store security officer pursued Chris during a shopping trip with his white wife, he found himself having to calm her when she almost exploded in anger at the mistreatment he encountered.

Not too long ago, my wife and I happened to be in a store where I was being followed by a security guard. I understood what the dynamics were and that I have to deal with this. My wife, on the other hand, wanted to pound them shitless. We had to process that experience 'cause that was her first real dealing with someone whom she loved having that experience. [Chris, 37, perceived as black]

Like Chris's wife, most white Americans have never dealt with such discrimination against themselves or persons close to them. When Chris and his wife married, knowingly or not, she entered a world in which discrimination is commonplace. Chris, on the other hand, must help his wife adjust to a life in which racial discrimination affects them both.

Other interviewees who appear black spoke of clerks turning nasty when they realized they were waiting on an interracial family. Janine vividly remembers facing a racially prejudiced and abusive salesperson while shopping with her white father when she was just twelve years old.

I was going holiday shopping with my dad and we went into an accessory store. When we went up to the register, my dad had the money. As I put the items down, the salesperson looked at me really strangely and then she asked my dad if she could help him. I said, "I'm purchasing things, he's going to pay for them." She's like, "Well, that's nice. What a kind stranger." I'm like, "No, he's my dad." She then said, "Oh, I'm so sorry. It's hard to tell who is with whom with these adoptions nowadays." By that time, my dad was turning absolutely red and he was really upset. He was trying to say he was going to pay for them, so we could leave. He said, "No, no, I'm her real father." She was like, "Oh." And then she got a really constipated look on her face. When we were leaving the store, she was saying to the ladies who worked in the store something about how people like my dad were "destroying the white race with these nigger babies." It was really just an awful comment. My dad didn't hear it, thank goodness, because he probably would have . . . I don't know, I don't know what he would have done. But it was really upsetting to me that someone could be just so ignorant. [Janine, 18, perceived as black]

Janine's example illustrates some white persons' aversion to interracial marriage. These whites believe that biracial children are a corrupting influence on the white race. This particular saleswoman's comments hark back to the days the "one drop rule" dominated society. At the heart of this rule was the popular Ku Klux Klan fear of the "mongrelization" of the races and ultimate decline of the white race due to the detrimental influence of black "blood." These white supremacists believe that members of the black and white races should avoid any type of social interaction.

While biracial persons who are perceived as black confront the same racial prejudices African Americans face, biracial Americans who appear white must also deal with racial discrimination. As noted in previous chapters, some white persons, who are unaware of biracial persons' African heritage, often speak disparagingly of blacks in their presence. Every interviewee who appeared white spoke of having and/or dreading such experiences.

Furthermore, when white-appearing biracial persons reveal their racial identity, many whites begin to treat them in a negative manner. Barbara, a forty-eight-year-old manager, discussed her own experience with this phenomenon.

I don't think that the question is how you appear. I think the question is where your head is and where other people's heads are when they see you, work with you, and know you. Being identified as a black person, forget your physical appearance, has a tremendous impact on how people react to what you say in meetings, whether they take you seriously or not, whether you're considered for a promotion, and whether you're deemed qualified or not. [Barbara, 48, perceived as white]

Barbara believes that, regardless of appearance, if racist persons become aware of a person's black identity, they will treat him or her as they would any other African American—in a discriminatory fashion.

Interestingly, not one of the younger biracial persons who appear white shares Barbara's opinion that racial appearance does not matter. They have not encountered the racial animosity usually leveled at African Americans. However, only one of these interviewees believes she should not benefit from affirmative action designed to benefit persons historically disadvantaged due to their dark skin. The majority of white-looking interviewees believe they should be eligible for AA.

BIRACIAL PERSONS AND AFFIRMATIVE ACTION

The twenty-six interviewees who discussed affirmative action cover the gamut of attitudes toward AA programs. As the following figures indicate (Table 7.1), the large majority favor such programs, but several others expressed mixed feelings and a smaller number oppose affirmative action.

Table 7.1
Interviewees' Attitudes Towards Affirmative Action

View on Affirmative Action	Overall
Pro-AA and in favor of biracial persons qualifyiing	58%
Mixed feelings about AA but believe all biracial persons should qualify	23%
Pro-AA but unsure whether or not biracial persons who appear white should qualify	4%
Pro-AA but believe biracial persons who appear white should not qualify	4%
Opposed to AA but believe biracial persons should qualify as long as it exists	11.5%

Given the size of the sample, no clear correlation can be made between the racial appearance of the respondents and their view of affirmative action. Of the interviewees who spoke about AA, three of the six who appear white, three of the six who are perceived as mixed racial, and nine of the fourteen who are viewed as black favor affirmative action programs and believe biracial persons should qualify.

Many of the other interviewees, opposed or unsure about AA, echoed the points of the black intellectuals opposed to affirmative action. Several mentioned they cannot help but wonder if the college of their choice accepted them merely because they help fill a racial diversity quota. These biracial students question their own qualifications and sense that their classmates also wonder about their academic ability. For some, this unease leads to their questioning the merits of affirmative action. For instance, Carol is unsure of whether she supports affirmative action because of the inferiority label that comes from being a minority student on a campus with an AA program.

I have mixed feelings about it. Sometimes I wonder, "Why am I at Baker College?" Is it because I was a fully merited student who deserved to come here, or is it because I was filling a quota because affirmative action is in place? It's not good for the psyche when you really think about why you are here. I wonder if I am just here to make the picture-perfect school. That's one of the things that I don't like about it. You never know if you're fully qualified. [Carol, 21, perceived as black]

Other interviewees who are college students spoke of sensing that the white students on campus view them as beneficiaries of preferential treatment.

Affirmative action really undermines the confidence of people who do end up somewhere. Because really there is a whole kind of undercurrent here about whether black students get in because they're black and because we need black people here. But it's the same thing with football players. Football players get in because they're football players. But the football players don't seem to have such a chip on their shoulder because of it. I don't know. I mean, I'm not strongly in opposition to it. I'm not sure how I feel about it. It's difficult. I'm definitely sitting on the fence. [Stacy, 18, perceived as black]

When Stacy declares that football players "get in because they are football players" she recognizes that affirmative action has always existed in one form or another, whether institutionalized or not. Students who play football and other members of the campus body, however, seem to have less of a problem with preferential treatment for athletes than they do with affirmative action for black students.[7] Perhaps because they sense this unease directed toward them, many African American students feel uncomfortable with a race-specific, as opposed to, say, an athletically based, affirmative action program.

Janine has also felt uneasy about her acceptance to college and her own talents because of the negative atmosphere surrounding affirmative action.

I think right now there is a big stigma attached to affirmative action for minority students. It's really hard. Like I know when I first came to Redwood I felt it. Every freshman has experiences doing badly in a class or being worried about how they are fitting in or whatever. And it's really easy to attach those anxieties to the skin color that all of a sudden you are noticing on your body. So, in that respect, I don't like affirmative action because it makes it too easy for people to point fingers at race to explain why a student isn't doing well. [Janine, 18, perceived as black]

Confronted with typical freshman insecurities coupled with a realization that she may have been a beneficiary of affirmative action, Janine began to "all of a sudden" notice her skin color. It took the negative repercussions of affirmative action for her to deem her pigmentation a sign of inferiority.

Jeanne, another college student, goes so far as to say that affirmative action is a tool of white supremacists. She maintains that liberal racists take comfort in the fact that affirmative action enables them to "help" black persons while at the same time publicly labeling them inferior.

I think affirmative action feeds an attitude that blacks in particular are inferior and need to have special help to do things. And so I would imagine that in some sense people who are by nature racist would like that because it's like, "Well, we can give them this because we can afford to give them this. But it is just a gift, it's charity we're doing for them because we're better off than they are and we'll help them a little." It's a way in which people who normally consider themselves liberal also satisfy a need to feel superior. [Jeanne, 18, perceived as white]

According to Jeanne, liberals have their cake and eat it too. They can publicly help black persons while at the same time soothe their sense of superiority by rationalizing that successful African Americans have "made it" thanks to their largesse.

Opinions and feelings aside, it is clearly true that some colleges accept certain minority students in order to fill their goals for racial diversity. One interviewee, initially rejected by the college of her choice, was eventually accepted when her racial background was considered.

It felt like in a large way that I got into Baker 'cause the admissions counselor set it up. I went and met with him and he pulled another admissions counselor into the room and said, "How did an African American student with these boards not get in?" I was like, "Excuse me!? [laughs] Why does that make a difference?" [Kimberly, 24, perceived as white]

While appalled that her racial background played a role in her acceptance, Kimberly has nevertheless benefited from affirmative action. Racial preference may not be palatable, but it is powerful. Of course, if Kimberly's parents had donated a large sum of money to Baker, the admissions counselors might have had the same conversation, simply exchanging the term "African American student" for "donor's daughter."

If Kimberly's father or mother had attended the school, she would be eligible for yet another unofficial form of affirmative action. She could have become a "legacy." A white male suburban college student at Stanford University described how he benefited from preferential treatment because his father attended the university. As he put it, his "chances of admission to [that] prestigious university were double that of the average applicant." Around campus, he and his fellow sons and daughters of alumni are known as "'legacies,' and according to the Stanford admissions office, [they] make up 14 percent of the undergraduate student body" [Thompson, 10/19/96:C1].

The idea of *race* as a determinant of preference has upset many persons, however. Steve, a young interviewee, agrees with those who believe that affirmative action is "reverse racism" and creates a new set of victims. He resents receiving an award over his white friends due to his racial background.

I may be the only black person I know who thinks this way, but I don't like affirmative action. It's reverse discrimination. That's a clichéd term now, but that's what I feel it is. A lot of my friends who got around what I did or even higher on the SATs didn't get any kind of award, but I did just 'cause I was black. Well, I didn't get a lot of money for it or win the Black National Merit Finalist or anything, but it still looks better on my college applications than not having won an award. I'd rather achieve for what I do rather than who I am. That's just the kind of person I am. [Steve, 18, perceived as black]

Steve does not want any part of a system that gives preferential treatment to him because of his race. He has no desire to fill a quota.

Unlike Steve, Joe, himself a beneficiary of affirmative action, maintains that quotas are necessary. While Steve resents receiving an award based on his race, Joe recalls centuries of racial discrimination in which African Americans were denied equal treatment because of the color of their skin. To him, affirmative action, quotas and all, is the only way black persons will have the opportunity to obtain parity with white Americans.

You know, affirmative action to me is about opportunity. All I needed was the opportunity, and I dare anybody to say that I'm less than qualified because of affirmative action. In this day and age, the sad thing about it all is that people associate affirmative action with being unqualified, and the very reason that affirmative action was written was because qualified people of color were not being granted access. That is the whole reason it was written. [Joe, 28, perceived as black]

According to Joe, true opportunity in the job market comes only with an affirmative action plan that includes goals and timetables. Employers have discriminated against black Americans in the workplace throughout U.S. history—he does not trust that "good faith" efforts will curb this practice now.

Chris, who lived through the Civil Rights Movement, agrees. He believes that affirmative action is necessary to ensure racial parity in the workforce.

I think there needs to be a program of equity. Because we're dealing with inequities that have existed for three hundred years. And somehow the Civil Rights Act of 1964 doesn't change anything. And it doesn't bother me in the least. I get more disturbed by people who abuse it. Those agencies who may hire someone because they need to find somebody, not because they're looking to provide quality service. That annoys me. But the idea, and the theory behind it, doesn't bother me in the least. [Chris, 37, perceived as white]

While Chris becomes irritated at companies who are not selective in their hiring of minority candidates, he believes a program that mandates that they do hire non white employees is essential. He maintains that equality of opportunity established by the 1964 Civil Rights Act is simply not enough to ensure minority employment.

Joe, raised in a poor family and now a member of the middle class, speaks loudly and clearly in support of affirmative action. He maintains that the racist nature of this society makes affirmative action necessary.

I think America should be embarrassed by the fact that affirmative action even exists because what it says to America is "we know you can't do it on your own, so we have to force you to do it." And these attacks on affirmative action sort of surprise me. White women have benefited from affirmative action more than African Americans, so if we want to review it in that sense, I'm all for it. Nobody ever says that white women are unqualified. It's always African Americans, regardless of gender. [Joe, 28, perceived as black]

Aside from pointing out the necessity of AA programs to ensure racial equity, Joe argues that white women, as well as racial minorities, benefit from affirmative action. He, like several other interviewees, maintain that white women have achieved disproportional gains from affirmative action without facing the backlash minorities encounter. Joe's comments indicate the lack of a strong union between beneficiaries of affirmative action: women and racial minorities do not show a unified stance on the issue.

Like Joe, Barbara is an avid supporter of affirmative action. She speaks as a black person rather than a woman when she discusses AA,[8] pointing out that certain groups of people have always received preferential treatment. Just as Stacy pointed out that her school gives priority to football players, in schools and companies across the country, Barbara notes that persons are admitted, hired, or promoted for a multitude of reasons other than mere qualifications.

Affirmative action exists in many ways, shapes, and forms that benefit other groups, but nobody calls it "affirmative action." And so it's kind of ridiculous to remove it where black people are concerned. For instance, why do you have an Academy Award for the best actress and the best actor? Why don't you just have the best performance award? Because they're giving women and men each a chance. That's affirmative action. Why do they have a prize for the best doctorate in sociology and another one for the best doctorate in chemistry? That's affirmative action. Nobody can tell me that the best educational institutions in America don't have affirmative action for rich donors' kids and legacies. There's a place set aside for those people to benefit [that is] special and different from others. So, when it comes to the one vehicle—educational and job opportunities—that has proven success in moving black people out of poverty, crime, and inner-city downward cycles, why would we want to stop that when this country is going straight down the toilet because of those social problems? I think affirmative action is great. I think Clarence Thomas is a big liar when he says it doesn't do anything and he didn't benefit. He's a total, big liar. If we hadn't had affirmative action, the upper middle-class blacks never would have been created and there wouldn't be a first generation of corporate executives that were black in America. There just wouldn't. [Barbara, 48, perceived as white]

Barbara herself is a beneficiary of affirmative action. A scholarship program designed to benefit exceptional minority business students paid for her MBA and a large company federally mandated to establish and maintain an affirmative action program hired her as a manager. Her educational and professional achievements would be entirely different had she not participated in AA programs.

According to Steinberg, "the occupational spheres where blacks have made the most progress—in government service, in major blue-collar occupations, in corporate management, and in the professions—are all areas where vigorous affirmative action programs have been in place over the past two decades." Without affirmative action, neither middle-class black firefighters and police officers nor upper middle-class black professional persons such as Barbara would exist. Destroying affirmative action now signals a clear retreat in the drive for racial parity in employment [1995:167].

Should Biracial People Qualify for Affirmative Action?

As previously stated, twenty-four of the twenty-six interviewees who spoke about affirmative action believe that biracial people should qualify for affirmative action. In our monoracially based racial structure, biracial Americans are eligible for all AA programs designated for racial minorities. If they appear black, they also, as seen above, face the same racial discrimination with which African Americans must deal. On the other hand, those who do not appear black may avoid much racial discrimination but have to endure hearing hurtful racial remarks made in their presence.

Jeanne's response to the question of whether biracial persons should qualify for affirmative action is typical.

I think if biracial people are going to be considered black in other circumstances, in sort of negative circumstances, they certainly should be able to take advantage of the positive aspects of it. Although it is no longer a legal thing, the one drop rule still applies. It's a social tradition, but it's there. [Jeanne, 18, perceived as white]

Most interviewees maintain that since biracial persons face many, if not all, of the discrimination black people encounter, they should qualify for affirmative action. It makes sense to Jeanne and to the vast majority of other interviewees that if society perceives a biracial person to be black then the biracial man or woman should receive all the benefits due a black person in this race-based society.

Other interviewees, like Barbara, believe that biracial persons should qualify for affirmative action even if they appear white. These interviewees maintain that even white-appearing biracial persons will be treated as black if their true racial identity is known. Therefore, all biracial persons, no matter what their appearance, should qualify for affirmative action.

As mentioned earlier, however, two younger interviewees are not convinced that biracial persons who appear white should qualify for affirmative action. Sarah, perceived as white herself, does not believe that persons who appear white should be eligible for AA. She maintains that racial appearance sharply defines what life experiences one encounters.

It depends on what your skin color is. In my sociology class, the professor split us up into groups. He put all the colored people into one group and all the white people in another group.[9] We then went over this list that some person wrote in a paper on all the advantages she has by being white that she didn't realize. The thing is, even though I'm Cape Verdian, I'm not oppressed because I don't have dark skin. So, I don't feel any of those racial pressures. Even if a person has one white parent and one black parent, if they have dark skin, then they will feel oppressed. They probably will experience some prejudice, whereas I don't. [Sarah, 19, perceived as white]

Because she appears white and therefore does not encounter racial prejudice and discrimination, Sarah does not believe she should qualify for affirmative action. As Janet, twenty-six, who describes herself as appearing Hispanic, states: "If a biracial person can fool everybody into thinking that she's white, then she wouldn't need affirmative action." However, if the biracial person makes a conscious effort to "fool" others, he or she must then deal with all the repercussions that come from "passing" as someone without any African ancestry, such as separation from family and constant fear of exposure.

As noted in Chapter 3, few young biracial adults choose to pass as either black or white. The majority of the interviewees who discussed racial classification forms favor the creation of some sort of multiracial category. Eighty-one percent of the interviewees who discussed the topic[10] want the Census to allow them to note all sides of their racial heritage. Four of the twenty-seven propose dismantling all racial demarcations, while one interviewee believes we should maintain the present racial classification system.

BIRACIAL PERSONS AND MULTIRACIAL CATEGORIES

While Project RACE advocates a sophisticated new racial categorization system that would recognize the unique racial backgrounds of multiracial persons, the Census and the Office of Management and Budget are also considering adding just a single multiracial box, with no subcategories on the Census 2000. Kim discussed the confusion that could result in mixed-race persons of various racial heritages being confined to one box.

A multiracial person could be someone who has an Asian parent and black parent, as well as somebody with a white parent and a black parent. There are so many different categories, to just throw everybody into one big bin like [laughs] they're all the same is hard for me. Because we're not. Personally, I would rather be able to define specifically who I am. [Kim, 33, perceived as black]

Kim, like most interviewees, does not want to move from one racial box that only describes half of her ancestry to one that leaves her entire racial background ambiguous.

As biracial adults begin to have children, the situation becomes even more complicated. Janet, who has children with a Hispanic man, understands this.

Eventually I would prefer that the racial labels be gone. One reason being I'm black and white and my children's father is Hispanic. What do you call that? [laughs]. And if they grow up and márry somebody who's Asian or mixed even more, what will their children be? I just think that America is the great melting pot. It's meant to mix up a little bit here and there. We should just be Americans. [Janet, 26, perceived as Hispanic]

Barbara would also like to see the whole racial classification system abolished. She says she could not care less about the struggle to add a multiracial box to the Census. She would like to see all racial categories abolished. "I don't care because I'm still in somebody's box. Why do I have to be in any box?" While her view may seem radical in a race-based nation such as the United States, the movement to abolish racial categorization is growing.

Susan believes that it is high time to abolish the very idea of race. One means of doing so is to eliminate all racial categories. She, like Barbara and Janet, opposes all such categories, including the proposed multiracial one. In Susan's eyes, a multiracial box actually contributes to the unnatural power of race. She uses a story to illustrate her feelings about the current debate over racial classifications.

You know when a little kid tells a lie? Somebody comes along and does something and you say, "Oh my gosh, what happened to such and such?" And the little kid will say, "Well . . ." And they'll make up a story and you can see the holes in the story, right? And you start trying to get them to confess by giving them opportunities for telling the truth, but instead they just keep telling a different story and a different story. Pretty soon you have this enormous story. If you do not ever stop and say, "You know, this whole story is a lie," you find yourself in a position of relating to this child in a way that is totally based on this lie. And if you decide confronting the child is not worth it and you walk away from it, you perpetually have to deal with that child on the basis of that particular incident when he or she lied. You know it's a lie, they know it's a lie, but nobody ever tells the truth about it. To add a box that says biracial is to perpetuate the lie. The honest response, the elimination of the lie, is to get rid of the boxes that say race or, if necessary, to put continents on and say "check all that apply." If we really need to have this kind of information, that's how we should do it. [Susan, 46, perceived as white]

Susan advocates facing the truth that race is meaningless and abolishing racial classifications. She does, however, believe in affirmative action. Her idea to substitute continents for race is her nod to the necessity of classifications. Interestingly, all four interviewees who wish to do away with racial classifications support affirmative action. This typifies the complexities and the realities of trying to alleviate the importance of race in a race-based society.

CONCLUSION

The transformation of racial identity among biracial Americans has profoundly affected this nation. Its repercussions rebound from individual biracial persons to the racial structures of our society. The change in racial identification on one level encourages corresponding alterations on the other.

Biracial Americans today face choices in racial identity never available to preceding generations. Now the nation must adjust to their growing resolve to identify with both sides of their racial heritage. But what does this mean for our traditionally monoracial society?

Janet's vision that "we should just be Americans" is full of potential. However, we must not forget the legacy of racism in the United States. In a society historically structured by racial considerations, what does it mean to "just be American?" Is it possible for the United States to become a nation in which race is not significant? Could this finally be the time when Americans unmask the social construction of race? Three centuries after plantation owners started to spread the concept of white racial superiority throughout the colonies to justify slavery, is America ready to discard the notion that race matters?

In this century, we have moved from interpretations of race based on the one drop rule toward one based entirely on racial appearance. We must not now seek a compromise position between the two means of constructing race. The issue is not to find some middle ground on the continuum but to discard it entirely, while remaining mindful of our discriminatory racial past.

Barring a crisis-charged racial backlash, race mixing appears irrepressible in the United States. The question is how long it will take monoracial Americans to come to terms with this inevitability. How long will white Americans be fearful of their son or daughter marrying a black person or even a biracial one? When will African Americans cease to dread the siphoning off of their numerical power by biracial Americans who wish to claim their white, as well as their black, racial heritage?

These concerns will abate when the present racial structure in the United States dissolves. By their very existence, biracial and multiracial Americans challenge this monoracial system. As their numbers grow, the legitimacy of our racial classification system shrivels. The demise of the present racial hierarchy is inevitable. Its replacement, however, is uncertain.

It is up to all Americans—monoracial and mixed racial—to work together to resist replacing today's racial hierarchy with another. While racial appearance will no doubt be of great influence in a society transitioning from a system based on official racial classification, it is important to avoid adopting new methods of racial demarcation that resemble the "brown paper bag" or "comb" test. We must strive to create a society in the next millennium in which neither race nor racial appearance indicates social class standing, a nation in which the need for affirmative action no longer exists.

In a country in which race and class have always been closely correlated, the challenge is great. We have much to inspire us, however. Rapidly increasing numbers of interracial couples prove that racial boundaries are neither impenetrable nor necessarily permanent. Their children teach us that race can be interpreted in multiracial, rather than merely monoracial, terms. This transformation of identity among biracial Americans reveals the fluidity and subjectivity of race.

The question "but what about the children?" now has a resoundingly positive answer. The children are fine. The overwhelming majority of young biracial adults feel fortunate to have both black and white ancestry. The fact that the question continues to be asked says more about the larger society than it does about biracial persons. Perhaps the response to such a query should be another question, "Why do you ask?"

In order to ensure a society in which we can all "just be American," we must now do as Patricia Raybon so eloquently suggests:

It's time . . . to start living up to our collective and individual potential as a blessed human community. We must start making connections, not just by race or age or gender or in other affiliate ways, but by linking our talents and energy, our resources, our ideas, our hopes—so we can finally, blessedly, banish our fears. Indeed, we must start loving so we can start living. And the past? It is over. [1996:136,137]

The United States will never again be a predominantly white monoracial society. This fact can either bring us closer together or tear us further apart. No matter what the outcome, though, one thing is certain regarding our monoracial past: it is over. Our multiracial future is at hand.

NOTES

1. Like many Americans, I find myself torn concerning affirmative action. While I believe it is a useful tool to achieve racial parity, I also contend that there are many negative repercussions to such programs. Many persons in power need to be prodded to hire racial minorities and women in proportion to their numbers in the greater population. However, the preferences given to these groups of persons in order to achieve this parity encourage resentment among white males and feelings of inferiority among those eligible for affirmative action. My greatest qualms about affirmative action, though, focus on the band-aid effect it has. While it has done much to create a black middle class, it does not address the needs of the most needy Americans. Moreover, it creates the impression that all racial minorities and women receive preferential treatment. This mistaken image contributes to the popular resentment and disparagement of impoverished uneducated persons of color who have not been given the opportunity to attain the skills needed to benefit from affirmative action.

2. The OMB is now undertaking extensive tests of alternative racial and ethnic categorizations in an attempt to meet "the Federal Government's many needs for data on race and ethnicity, while at the same time providing categories and definitions that are readily understood and generally accepted by the public. . . . This review process is scheduled to be completed by mid-1997 so that changes, if any, in the racial and ethnic categories can be implemented in the 2000 census" [Office of Management and Budget,

1997:42–44].

3. Ohio, Illinois, Georgia, Indiana, and Michigan have passed legislation establishing a multiracial category on racial classification forms. Project RACE has also persuaded North Carolina and Florida school districts to include a multiracial category on all school forms. In 1995, the ACT Scholastic Test added a multiracial classification [Project RACE web-site (http://www/projectrace.mindspring.com) and personal conversation with Susan Graham].

4. This information was garnered from a personal conversation with Graham on 10/23/96.

5. Public education by the OMB and the Census must accompany such a change in the racial classification form. This would both ensure that all Americans have a clear understanding of their racial and ethnic categorization options (and the implications of each) and increase their comfort with choosing a new category. The multiracial movement should also play a large role in this education process. This campaign to explain the new form could be a great means of recruiting more members for the multiracial movement and increasing the strength of the organization.

6. This information is based on personal observation and a conversation with Susan Graham. While not an organization devoted to protest rallies or marches, Project RACE did agree to participate in the rally. When the group realized that Byrd's organization efforts would result in a sparse turnout, Project RACE separated itself from any close connection with the event. They did, however, effectively use the rally as a springboard for a bone marrow drive that they organized. Byrd did not return phone messages asking him to discuss the rally.

7. Of course, in many instances, these populations overlap. Among those interviewed, however, only one received a substantial scholarship due to his athletic skills. While in the instance of this one interviewee, it is ambiguous whether his athletic ability assisted his entrance into the college of his choice, clearly, the vast majority of interviewees did not receive preferential treatment due to excellence in sports.

8. During the interview, I pointedly asked Barbara whether she was speaking first as a woman or a black person when she spoke of affirmative action. She replied that she was speaking as a black person. Throughout the interview, it was clear to me that, in Barbara's hierarchy of identities, her identity as a black person outranks her identity as a female.

9. Her professor carefully took her aside and explained that he was assigning her to the "white" group because of her appearance but that she was free to move to the other group if and when she wished. Sarah concurred with her professor that she belonged in the "white" group.

10. Twenty-seven interviewees discussed the possible creation of a multiracial category on the Census.

Appendix: Notes on Methodology

TALES FROM THE FRONT LINES OF RESEARCHING: THE STRUGGLE TO FIND INTERVIEWEES

My experience finding interviewees reflects the changing demographics of the biracial population. I started the interview process by placing ads in college newspapers. The response was rewarding. A combination of ads in college newspapers, personal contacts, and the snowball effect enabled me to fill my sampling goal of interviewees under the age of thirty rather quickly and easily.

Finding biracial persons over the age of thirty was much more difficult. Not only is the population relatively small, it is almost impossible to locate. I did not want to rely on the few interracial organizations that exist because I was seeking a more representative sample of older black-white Americans. Utilizing members of mixed racial organizations would limit me to those who identify as biracial. According to virtually all past studies, the majority of biracial Americans over the age of thirty are living as black persons, not persons who are both black and white. The racial identity of older black-white persons is less ambiguous than that of younger biracial Americans. The vast majority were raised as exclusively black. Throughout their youth, the "one drop rule" reigned unchallenged.

In spite of this evidence and my initial resignation to rely heavily on secondary data for this older group of biracial Americans, I made every effort to find biracial persons over thirty to interview. I wanted to explore for myself this scarcely traversed realm. In doing so, I opened myself to finding older biracial Americans who identified as something other than black—persons whom other researchers may have assumed nonexistent.

Time and time again, I asked persons if they knew anyone over the age of thirty who has both a black and a white parent to be met with the response, "I don't know anyone over thirty, but my neighbor/brother/sister/cousin/friend has little children who are biracial." Evidently, the biracial baby boom is stronger than ever. Researchers interested in interviewing young biracial children will have no problem finding potential interviewees.

Interestingly, and to my great frustration, on more than one occasion I interviewed persons who did not have black and white racial heritage. In one instance, a young woman answering my ad explained she was biracial and requested an interview. During the interview she explained that she was Jewish and white. In her eyes that made her biracial. It did not, however, make one of her parents black and one white. From that moment on, I vowed to quiz potential interviewees on the phone to ensure that they truly were offspring of an African American and a white parent. I let my guard down, however, when a close colleague of mine volunteered a biracial friend for me to interview. Having discussed, at great length, my book topic with this colleague, I assumed that the person whom he directed me to was, indeed, the offspring of both a black and a white parent. It was with great surprise that I learned during the interview that the person my colleague had encouraged me to interview was the offspring of an African American and a Native American.

Aside from resulting in two discarded interviews, these experiences of mistaken racial identity reveal pertinent aspects of racial identity today. The problems I encountered with misinterpreted cases of identity mirror the increasing fluidity and ambiguity of racial identity. Race is no longer obvious. Researchers of race today must deal with the increasing vagueness of racial identity.

As my search for interviewees continued, I bored relatives, friends, and casual acquaintances with descriptions of persons whom I was seeking in hopes they could suggest someone they knew. When several activist black ministers said, "No, sorry, I don't know anyone and I'm not sure you'll be able to find any. Good luck." I began to grow a little concerned.

That these ministers did not know of any biracial persons in their congregations surprised me. Ministers are an integral part of the African American community. I can only imagine that one's racial identity is not a subject of speculation for black congregations; they accept as black without question all those who identify as black. Because the vast majority of the African American population has mixed-race heritage, black-white biracial persons are not necessarily obvious in black churches. While biracial children may be noticeable in a black church because of the attendance of their parents, older biracial persons who visit the church without their parents are probably assumed to be black. Eventually, I garnered only five of my over-thirty interviewees by relying on the assistance of those I knew.

One memorable attempt to enlist the help of the most casual of acquaintances occurred when I was seated with a group of much older persons, whom I had never met before, at an awards banquet. While most of the conversation was rather dull, one woman's story of how she was shocked and horrified to find that someone whom she had told a racist joke to was actually half black sparked my interest.

When the polite laughter of my tablemates died down, I proceeded to tell her, "I am writing my book on racial identity among biracial persons, and do you happen to remember the name of the person you described in your story?" Flustered and bewildered at my request, she said she could not recall the name of the person by whose race she had been so startled. Presumably, they did not keep in touch after that episode. "Oh well," I told her, "it was worth a shot." My desperation was growing. I had been reduced to asking white people relaying racist jokes for their assistance in finding older biracial persons!

Fortunately, an ad I placed in the Boston-based black newspaper elicited a few responses. Of this group of over-thirty interviewees, each of the three over forty identified as black and described similar tales of racial identity formation. Interestingly, though, of the five interviewees in their thirties, two identified as black, two self-defined as both black and white, and one declared himself to be interracial.

The interviews in the secondary sources I utilized of biracial persons born before the Movement corroborated the results of my sample. Of the twenty-two secondary interviews used, nine of the ten interviewees over forty identified as black, while only six of the twelve interviewees in their thirties self-defined as black. Of the other six, five identified as biracial, while one identified as both black and biracial. Therefore, while my findings support the research that indicates the vast majority of Americans with both an African American and a white parent born before 1965 racially identify as black, they also reveal the transformation in process. My relatively small sample of over-thirty interviewees provides evidence of both the effect of the "one drop rule" and the emergence of the transformation in racial identity.

I met my goal of finding biracial persons under thirty to interview with much greater ease. In fact, I surpassed my point of saturation. After approximately twenty interviews, steady and persistent patterns began to emerge in the tales of these biracial persons. I continued to conduct interviews for two reasons. First, there is a paucity of systematically analyzed data on biracial Americans. I thought it best to add to this small collection instead of turning away prospective interviewees. Second, by coincidence, the last person referred to me brought my number of interviews to forty. By most accounts, forty appears to be a good number of interviews to include in a study such as this. Having reached both my inductive and marketable goals, I concluded my schedule of interviews.

DESIGN OF DATA COLLECTION

I collected the data for this book primarily through semistructured, intensive interviews of individuals who have both an African American and a white parent. The interviews ranged from one to three hours. I chose this type of data collection for several reasons. Discussions concerning race are always sensitive. This format enabled me to gain the trust and confidence of the biracial person being interviewed. This, I believe, made it possible for me to gather more honest and elaborate answers than I could using another methodology, such as a survey.

The semistructured format also allowed me to compare answers to questions asked of each interviewee and pursue topics of interest initiated by the various interviewees. This further enabled me to fine-tune my focus when needed and achieve a greater depth of understanding of the process of racial identity formation among biracial individuals. I believe that these "pluses" outweigh the inevitable "minuses" of intensive interviews (e.g., relatively small, nonprobability sample, lack of standardization, possibility of interviewer bias).

I based the coding and analysis of the interviews on the grounded theory approach discussed by Glaser and Strauss [1967]. While I had some tentative hypotheses going into the data collection based upon a review of secondary data sources, historical knowledge, and personal observation, I was open to whatever findings the data elicited. I derived my theories from my analyses of the data. This type of approach allowed me to be receptive to ideas I had not considered before conducting the research.

As a secondary source of data, I also utilized a survey of college students. Two hundred and four college students responded to the following question:

Should those who have both an African American and a white parent be racially classified as

A) WHITE   B) BLACK   or   C) BIRACIAL? *(Circle One)*
If you are unsure which to circle, write why you are uncertain.

These students were enrolled at New England-area colleges. The data derived from this question enabled me to discover how young, educated people today racially define biracial Americans. While the colleges utilized for this survey are situated in two New England states, many of the students at these schools come from states outside New England. Therefore, the survey results do not indicate solely a New England point of view on racial identity. I plan to expand this sample to cover a broader spectrum of the U.S. population, including older and less-educated Americans.

The surveys were dispersed and then collected in a classroom situation. I enlisted the aid of two professors who conducted the survey during their classes. The survey was directed in this manner in order to ensure a very high and rapid return rate. Two hundred and fifteen surveys were handed out with a completion rate of 94.8 percent. As discussed in Chapter 4, 15.2 percent of those who returned the survey refused to respond to the question for various reasons that they wrote out on the survey form. The reasons for not responding ranged from "People should be able to choose for themselves" (57.9%) to "We shouldn't label people" (41.4%) to "It depends on the appearance of the individual" (.6%). This affirmed for me the current "backlash" against racial classifications.

SAMPLE OF INTERVIEWEES

As discussed earlier, I interviewed forty biracial adults, basing the number of interviewees primarily on the point of saturation. Included in the sample of interviewees were persons with a cross section of economic, racial features, and parental backgrounds. Young adults who are students at (or who have recently graduated from) Boston-area colleges comprised the majority of the subsample of biracial persons born after 1965 (the culmination of the Civil Rights Movement). While all but two persons in this sample attend or recently graduated from college, there is reason to believe that this group represents a large portion of the biracial population. According to Spickard [1989], most of the black/white interracial marriages in this century have occurred in the middle and professional classes. The biracial offspring of these marriages, therefore, comprise a section of the population that is highly likely to receive a college education. Focusing on college students provided a relatively easy means of communication with the targeted population by advertisements in student newspapers. This group represents the most recent generation of mixed-race adults. Examining their perspective provided a glimpse into the future of biracial-monoracial relations in the United States.

While limited in many ways, the biracial college student population is more economically diverse than most samples of students attending costly schools with very good academic reputations. Because biracial students are considered to be a minority (usually black rather than biracial), some of those I interviewed attend college through the benefit of a minority scholarship. Therefore, even though the majority of biracial adults are offspring of financially comfortable parents, the individuals in this sample come from a cross section of economic backgrounds. This made it possible to examine the effect of economic class on racial identity formation while having the subsample predominantly[1] limited to those who attend, or have attended, rather prestigious/expensive colleges.[2]

As is the norm in the majority of studies that depend on volunteers, achieving an equitable sex ratio was difficult. Women are more likely to volunteer their time than are men. I managed to achieve a fair degree of parity between the sexes, however. Thirty-eight percent, fifteen of the forty interviewees, were male.

As alluded to above, convenience sampling was the sampling method utilized. The student population consisted primarily of those individuals who answered the following advertisement placed in selected college newspapers:

Two movie passes will be given to those who have both an African American and a white parent and will be interviewed for a doctoral dissertation. Call Kathleen (Ph.D. candidate, Boston College) ***–****.

I (and others interviewing people for a book)[3] believe the prospect of receiving movie passes provides a good rationalization and motivation for people to participate in the study. Almost all of those I interviewed expressed genuine delight at receiving them. If I had not advertised a "reward" for those who agreed to an interview, those who would have volunteered would most likely be limited to those who enjoy discussing and reflecting on their racial identity. The prospect of receiving movie passes prompted many interviewees who had not thought much about their racial identity to contact me for an interview. It also indicated that I was serious about the interview process and valued their time and stories. Although a pair of movie passes costs only nine dollars, they were a powerful symbol. They demonstrated that I appreciated both my subject matter and my interviewees enough to make an investment in each interview. It was clear that the respondents appreciated the symbolism of the movie passes as much as their monetary value and usefulness.

I also used the snowball method effectively for this cohort of interviewees. Fellow interviewees referred three members of this group to me and I used my own personal contacts to find six other under-thirty interviewees. In each of these latter cases, a combination of personal persuasion and the anticipation of receiving two movie passes worked to encourage persons to agree to an interview.

As previously described, the second group of interviewees consisted of biracial individuals who were born in or before 1965. The addition of these interviewees enabled me to compare the development of racial self-definition among biracial Americans born before the full enactment of the Civil Rights laws with the racial identity formation of biracial Americans born after the Movement. This comparison illustrates the transformation of racial identity.

There are several reasons for my difficulty in finding older biracial individuals to participate in this study. Demographically, there are fewer older biracial adults. It is more difficult to pinpoint areas in which older biracial adults may live than it is to find biracial college students in the Boston area. The majority of college students read their school's student newspaper, while no corresponding vehicles of information for the post-college-age population of biracial adults exist.

I relied heavily on the snowball method and my own personal contacts in my efforts to find interviewees for this subsample of biracial persons over the age of thirty. I discovered five of this group through my personal contacts and word of mouth. Again, personal persuasion and the prospect of movie passes worked to entice this group of people to agree to an interview. The other three interviewees contacted me through the following pro bono ad I placed in a Boston-based African American newspaper:

Two movie passes will be given to those over thirty who have both an African American and a white parent and will be interviewed for a doctoral dissertation. Call Kathleen (Ph.D. candidate, Boston College) ***_****.

In using this method of recruitment, I ran the risk of finding only persons who identify as "black enough" to read an African American newspaper. This concern was offset by the fact that one of this group was informed of the advertisement by her black mother who reads the newspaper, while another identified as both black and biracial. In each case, the interviewee's connection with the black newspaper did not necessarily indicate a disconnection with their white heritage.

As mentioned previously, I also utilized secondary data analysis in my efforts to compare the racial identities of biracial people who were born before and after the enactment of Civil Rights legislation. Lise Funderburg's *Black, White, Other* [1994], a compilation of interviews with black-white biracial adults, was an excellent resource. In order to supplement my sample of interviews of biracial persons over thirty, I used twenty-two of her interviews. From her book, I selected those interviewees who clearly identified themselves racially and were over the age of thirty at the time of the interview. In all cases, the secondary data supported my original findings.

VALIDITY AND RELIABILITY

As in all research based on face-to-face interviews, the validity of the answers was easier to control for than their reliability. It is easier to ensure for validity using in-depth interviews than with other research methods, such as surveys. Because of my presence, I could ask a question in different ways until I was confident that the interviewee correctly understood the intent of the question before he or she responded to it. I could clarify responses through the use of probes. Because of my direct interaction with those being interviewed, I was able to discern each interviewee's level of comfort when answering questions. With this knowledge, I could reword or change the order of questions to ensure the greatest possible degree of candor from the individual being interviewed. Some interviewees needed to discuss relatively mundane issues about themselves before they could delve into often painful stories of their racial self-identification process. Other persons were eager to discuss such matters as soon as the interview began.

Reliability can be affected in a variety of ways. The methodology of in-depth interviews results in a lack of standardization. Another researcher would produce a different sample, and neither that group of respondents nor my own would be entirely representative. This is due to the convenience sampling method utilized and the natural variation of emphasis from one interview to the next. However, the fact that my group of respondents had a wide variety of racial features and came from diverse states, classes, and neighborhoods leads me to believe that another researcher conducting the same type of study would achieve similar results.

It is necessary to acknowledge, however, that my mood and the attitude of the interviewee may have resulted in a change in "climate" of the interview that could have affected its results. The "climate" could be affected in a number of ways. I might unconsciously have relayed to the interviewee my own views on the issues being discussed. It is probable that the fact that I am a white interviewer had some effect on the responses elicited. Each interviewee may have a different opinion and/or level of comfort level with my whiteness. This could have affected the level of candor of some of the interviewees' answers. My gender may have had a similar effect. Respondents may have hesitated to say something to me because I am a woman. Finally, the same questions might have elicited very different answers from a disgruntled, wary, and/or hurried interviewee than from one who was happy and talkative. It is important to note that in no case did I suspect that the responses of interviewees were compromised for any of the above reasons.

However, my race was raised as a concern by one person I interviewed. The one interviewee who requested I receive his formal permission before I used his interview in a publication refused to allow me to do so when I did ask him for that freedom. He decided, upon reflection, that I "did not ask the right questions." While acknowledging that my methodology was acceptable, he said that if I were biracial I "would have asked different questions." To my frustration, despite a lengthy discussion, he could not tell me what questions he would have preferred I ask. I left my meeting with him firmly believing that my race, rather than my questions, were at the base of his refusing me permission to use his interview in publications. I do not, however, believe that his interview was compromised because of his bias against my whiteness. He indicated that he spoke freely during the interview.

I could never have complete control over the temperament of the individuals I interviewed. However, at each encounter, I did strive to portray myself as a warm, interested, professional interviewer and make a consistent effort to make each interviewee comfortable. I also made every effort to ensure that my questions were free from bias and that the interviewees' responses were candid. In this way, I achieved the highest degree of reliability possible while using the methodology of in-depth interviews.

SUMMARY AND TABLES

In all, I interviewed forty biracial persons. I illustrate the racial identity of the respondents I personally interviewed in tables A.1 - 5. My results reflect that, among the variables of class, racial features, age, and sex, age is the most influential factor in the racial self-definition of black-white biracial Americans. The majority of biracial persons born before the Civil Rights Movement identify as exclusively black, while those born after the Civil Rights Movement declare both sides of their racial heritage. This is clear evidence of a transformation in racial identity from black to biracial among Americans with both an African American and a white parent.

Table A.1
Racial Identity By Sex

Racial Identity

		Black	White	Black and Biracial	Biracial	Does Not Identify Racial	
Sex	Males	46.6% (7)	0%	6.6% (1)	46.6%* (7)	0%	(n = 15)
	Females	32% (8)	0%	8% (2)	52%** (13)	8% (2)	(n = 25)

*One person in this group identifies as "all mixed up and Puerto Rican."
**One person in this group identifies as "half black."

Table A.2
Racial Identity by Economic Class

Racial Identity

		Black	White	Black and Biracial	Biracial	Does Not Identify Racial	
Class	Upper	66.6% (2)	0%	33.3% (1)	0%	0%	(n = 3)
	Upper Middle	11% (1)	0%	0%	77.7% (7)	11.1% (1)	(n = 9)
	Middle	42.1% (8)	0%	5.2% (1)	47.4%* (9)	5.2% (1)	(n = 19)
	Lower Middle	50% (2)	0%	0%	50% (2)	0%	(n = 4)
	Lower	40% (2)	0%	20%** (1)	40% (2)	0%	(n = 5)

*One person in this group identifies as "all mixed up and Puerto Rican."
**This person was originally raised in the lower class, but his/her family is now wealthy.

Table A.3
Racial Identity by Birth Cohort

Racial Identity

		Black	White	Black and Biracial	Biracial	Does Not Identify Racial	
Birth Cohort	Born after 1965	31.2% (10)	0%	3.1% (1)	59.3%* (19)	6.3% (2)	(n = 32)
	Born in or before 1965	62.5% (5)	0%	25% (2)	12.5% (1)	0%	(n = 8)

*One person in this group identifies as "all mixed up and Puerto Rican."

Table A.4
Racial Identity By Racial Appearance

Racial Identity

		Black	White	Black and Biracial	Biracial	Does Not Identify Racial	
Racial Appear-ance	Perceived as Black	38% (8)	0%	14.3% (3)	42.9% (9)	4.8% (1)	(n = 21)
	Perceived as White	20% (2)	0%	0%	70% (7)	10% (1)	(n = 10)
	Perceived as Mixed or Hispanic	55.6% (5)	0%	0%	44.4% (4)	0%	(n = 9)

Table A.5
Racial Identity By Racial Makeup of Childhood Neighborhood

Racial Identity

		Black	White	Black and Biracial	Biracial	Does Not Identify Racial	
Child- hood Neigh- borhood	Predom. White	26.3% (5)	0%	15.8% (3)	52.3% (10)	5.3% (1)	(n = 19)
	Predom. Black	60% (3)	0%	0%	40% (2)	0%	(n = 5)
	Diverse	43.8%** (7)	0%	0%	50%* (8)	6.3% (1)	(n = 16)

*One person in this group identifies as "all mixed up and Puerto Rican."
**One person in this group grew up in two neighborhoods throughout—a predominantly white neighborhood during summers and a predominantly black neighborhod during the school year.

NOTES

1. Aside from the two persons who did not achieve beyond a high school education, one under-thirty interviewee, whom I found through personal contacts, attends a community college.

2. While it was impossible to control for the level of education with this small sample, I have reason to believe that intelligence and knowledge varied considerably among the interviewees. While several appeared extremely intelligent, there were also a number who did not. One interviewee, despite attending a highly competitive college, was not familiar with the term "affirmative action." On at least one occasion, an interviewee confessed to me that she had no idea how she got into the college she was attending because her grades and SATs were both low. This indicates that some of these interviewees were accepted by prestigious colleges on the basis of their African heritage rather than their intellectual prowess or past educational achievements.

3. See James A. Vela-McConnell's methodology section in his dissertation, "Who Is My Neighbor?: Social Affinity in a Modern World," Boston College, 1997.

Bibliography

"Alabama Principle in Prom Strife Wins Election." *Boston Globe*, July 27, 1996, p. A15.

Asch, Solomon E. *Social Psychology*. Englewood Cliffs, N.J.: Prentice-Hall, 1952.

Associated Press. "Rally Held for Multiracial Category on 2000 Census." *Boston Globe*, July 21, 1996, p. A21.

Barzun, Jacques. *Race: A Study in Superstition*. New York: Harper & Row, 1965.

Baudrillard, Jean. *In the Shadows of the Silent Majorities*. New York: Semiotext(e), 1983.

Bennett, Lerone, Jr. *Before the Mayflower*. Chicago: Johnson Publishing Company, 1987.

Bergmann, Barbara R. *In Defense of Affirmative Action*. New York: Basic Books, 1996.

Bernstein, Nell. "Goin' Gangsta, Choosin' Cholita." *Utne Reader*, March/April 1995, pp. 87–90.

Berzon, Judith R. *Neither White or Black*. New York: New York University Press, 1978.

Blumer, Herbert. *Symbolic Interaction: Perspective and Method*. Englewood Cliffs, N.J.: Prentice-Hall, 1969.

Bouvier, Leon F. *Peaceful Invasions: Immigration and Changing America*. Lanham, Md.: University Press of America, 1992.

Bradshaw, Carla K. "Beauty and the Beast." Pp. 77–90 in *Racially Mixed People in America*, ed. Maria P. P. Root. Newbury Park, Calif.: Sage Publications, 1992.

Carter, Stephen L. *Reflections of an Affirmative Action Baby*. New York: Basic Books, 1991.

Cockburn, Alexander. "Oil's Sweet Music." *The Nation*, December 9, 1996, pp. 9–10.

Cohen, Carl. *Naked Racial Preference*. Lanham, Md.: Madison Books, 1995.

Cooley, Charles Horton. *Human Nature and the Social Order*. New York: Schocken Books, 1902.

Coombe, Rosemary J. "Tactics of Appropriation and the Politics of Recognition in Late Modern Democracies." *Political Theory* 21:411–33, August, 1993.

Coser, Lewis A. *Masters of Sociological Thought*. San Diego: Harcourt Brace Jovanovich, 1977.

Davis, James F. *Who Is Black?* University Park, Pa.: Pennsylvania State University Press, 1991.

Deaux, Kay. "Personalizing Identity and Socializing Self." Pp. 9–34 in *Social Psychology of Identity and the Self Concept*, ed. Glynis M. Breakwell. London: Surrey University

Press, 1992.

Derber, Charles. *The Wilding of America*. New York: St. Martin's Press, 1996.

Du Bois, W.E.B. *The Souls of Black Folk*. New York: Library of America, 1912/1990.

Erikson, Erik. "Ego Development and Historical Change." *Psychoanalytic Study of the Child*, 2:359–96, 1946.

Evans, Sarah. *Personal Politics*. New York: Vintage Books, 1979.

Featherstone, Mike. *Undoing Culture*. London: Sage Publications, 1995.

Fine, Gary Alan. "Symbolic Interactionism in the Post-Blumerian Age." Pp. 117–57 in *Frontiers of Social Theory: The New Synthesis*, ed. George Ritzer. New York: Columbia University Press, 1990.

Franklin, John Hope. *From Slavery to Freedom*. New York: Alfred A. Knopf, 1980.

Frazier, Franklin. *Brown Bourgeoisie*. New York: Collier Books, 1965.

Funderburg, Lise. *Black, White, Other*. New York: William Morrow and Company, 1994.

———. "Boxed In." *New York Times*, July 10, 1996, p. A15, col. 2.

Funding Federal Civil Rights Enforcement: A Report of the United States Commission on Civil Rights. The Commission [1995]: Washington, D.C., June 1995.

Gergen, Kenneth J. *The Saturated Self*. New York: Basic Books, 1991.

Gibbs, Jewelle Taylor. "Identity and Marginality." *American Journal of Orthopsychiatry* 57(2):265–78, April, 1987.

Gibbs, Jewelle Taylor and Alice M. Hines. "Negotiating Ethnic Identity: Issues for Black-White Biracial Adolescents." Pp. 212–228 in *Racially Mixed People in America*, ed. Maria P. P. Root. Newbury Park, Calif.: Sage Publications, 1992.

Glaser, Barney G., and Anselm L. Strauss. *The Discovery of Grounded Theory*. Chicago: Aldine Publishing Co., 1967.

———. *Status Passages*. Chicago and New York: Aldine Atherton, 1971.

Goffman, Erving. *Stigma*. Englewood Cliffs, N.J.: Prentice-Hall, 1963.

Goldberg, David Theo. *Racist Culture*. Cambridge, Mass.: Blackwell Publishers, 1993.

Goldsmith, William W., and Edward J. Blakely. *Separate Societies*. Philadelphia: Temple University Press, 1992.

Gordon, Milton M. *Assimilation in American Life*. New York: Oxford University Press, 1964.

Griffin, John Howard. *Black Like Me*. London and Glasgow: Collins Clear-Type Press, 1960.

Haizlip, Shirlee Taylor. *The Sweeter the Juice*. New York: Simon and Schuster, 1994.

Hampton, Henry, and Steve Fayer. *Voices of Freedom*. New York: Bantam Books, 1990.

Harding, Sandra. *Whose Science? Whose Knowledge?* Ithaca, N.Y.: Cornell University Press, 1991.

Harper, Frances E. W. *Iola Leroy, or Shadows Uplifted*. New York: Oxford University Press, 1892/1988.

Harrington, Walt. *Crossings*. New York: HarperCollins, 1992.

Henriques, Fernando. *Children of Conflict*. New York: E.P. Dutton and Company, 1975.

Horton, Carrell Peterson, and Jessie Carner Smith, eds. P. 5 in *Statistical Record of Black America*. Detroit, New York, London: Gale Research, 1990.

Hughes, C. Everett. *The Sociological Eye*. Chicago and New York: Aldine Atherton, 1971.

Hughes, Hampton. *The Ways of White Folks*. New York: Vintage Books, 1971.

Hughes, Michael, and Bradley R. Hertel. "The Significance of Color Remains: A Study of Life Chances, Mate Selection, and Ethnic Consciousness Among Black Americans." *Social Forces* 68 (4):1105–20, 1990.

Ignatiev, Noel. *How the Irish Became White*. New York and London: Routledge, 1995.

Johnson, James Weldon. *The Autobiography of an Ex-Coloured Man.* New York: Alfred A. Knopf, 1927.

Jones, Lisa. *Bulletproof Diva.* New York: Doubleday, 1994.

Jordan, Winthrop D. *White over Black.* Chapel Hill: University of North Carolina Press, 1968.

Kalmijm, Matthos. "Trends in Black/White Intermarriage." *Social Forces,* 72, (1):119–46, 1993.

Karp, David, and William C. Yoels. *Sociology in Everyday Life.* Itasca, Ill.: F. E. Peacock Publishers, 1993.

Kellner, Douglas. "The Postmodern Turn: Positions, Problems, and Prospects." Pp. 255–86 in *Frontiers of Social Theory.* ed. George Ritzer. New York: Columbia University Press, 1990.

––––––. "Popular Culture and the Construction of Postmodern Identities." Pp. 141–77 in *Modernity and Identity*, ed. Scott Lash and Jonathan Friedman. Cambridge, Mass.: Blackwell, 1992.

Kich, George Kitahara. "The Developmental Process of Asserting a Biracial, Bicultural Identity." Pp. 304–20 in *Racially Mixed People in America*, ed. Maria P. P. Root. Newbury Park, Calif.: Sage Publications, 1992.

Kinney, James. *Amalgamation!* Westport, Conn.: Greenwood Press, 1985.

Lal, Barbara Ballis. "Symbolic Interaction Theories." *American Behavioral Scientist* 38, (3):421–41, January, 1995.

Larsen, Nella. *Quicksand.* New York: Negro Universities Press, 1928.

––––––. *Passing.* New York: Negro Universities Press, 1929.

Leland, John, and Gregory Beals. "In Living Colors." *Newsweek*, May 5, 1997, pp. 58–60.

Lorber, Judith. *Paradoxes of Gender.* New Haven and London: Yale University Press, 1994.

Lyotard, Jean-Françoise. *The Postmodern Condition.* Minneapolis: University of Minnesota Press, 1984.

Marger, Martin N. *Race and Ethnic Relations.* Belmont, Calif.: Wadsworth Publishing Company, 1994.

Marriott, Michel. "Multiracial Americans Ready to Claim Their Own Identity." *New York Times*, July 20, 1996, p. A1.

Mathabane, Mark, and Gail Mathabane. *Love in Black and White.* New York: HarperCollins, 1992.

Mathews, Linda. "More than Identity Rides on New Racial Category." *New York Times*, August 6, 1996, p. A1, col.1.

McCall, George J., and J. L. Simmons. *Identities and Interactions.* New York: Free Press, 1966/1978.

McGrory, Brian. "Mixed Message." *Boston Globe*, May 21, 1995, p. A1.

Mead, George Herbert. *Mind, Self, and Society*, ed. Charles W. Morris. Chicago: University of Chicago Press, 1934.

Miller, Robin L. "The Human Ecology of Multiracial Identity." Pp. 24–36 in *Racially Mixed People in America*, ed. Maria P. P. Root. Newbury Park, Calif.: Sage Publications, 1992.

Mills, Candy. (Editorial) *Interrace.* December 1994/January 1995, p. 2.

Morganthau, Tom. "What Color Is Black? What Color Is White?" *Newsweek*, February 23, 1995, pp. 62–69.

Nakashima, Cynthia L. "An Invisible Monster: The Creation and Denial of Mixed Race People in America." Pp. 162–80 in *Racially Mixed People in America*, ed. Maria P. P. Root. Newbury Park, Calif.: Sage Publications, 1992.

Office of Management and Budget. "Statistical Programs of the United States Government," 1997:42–44.

Omi, Michael, and Howard Winant. *Racial Formation in the United States: From the 1960's to the 1980's*. New York: Routledge & Kegan Paul, 1986.

Park, Robert. *Race and Culture*. New York: Free Press, 1964.

———. "Human Migration and the Marginal Man." *American Journal of Sociology* 33 (6):881–93, May 1928.

———. "Personality and Cultural Conflict." *Publication of the American Sociological Society* 25:95–110, May 1931.

———. "Mentality of Racial Hybrids." *The American Journal of Sociology* 36:435–51, January 1931.

Pertman, Adam. "Affirmative Action at the Crossroads." *Boston Globe*, October 5, 1996, p. A1.

Project RACE web-site, Internet, 10/28/96. [http://www/projectrace.mindspring.com]

Rainwater, Lee, and William L. Yancey. *The Moynihan Report and the Politics of Controversy*. Cambridge, Mass.: MIT Press, 1967.

Raybon, Patricia. *My First White Friend*. New York: Viking Penguin, 1996.

Reuter, Edward. *The Mulatto in the United States*. New York: Negro Universities Press, 1918/1969.

———. *Race Mixture*. New York: Johnson Reprint Corp., 1930/1970.

Roberts, Craig Paul, and Lawrence M. Stratton. *The New Color Line*. Washington, D.C.: Regnery Publishing, 1995.

Roediger, David R. *The Wages of Whiteness: Race and the Making of the American Working Class*. London, New York: Verso, 1991.

Root, Maria P. P. "Within, between, and beyond Race." Pp. 3–11 in *Racially Mixed People in America*, ed. Maria P. P. Root. Newbury Park, Calif.: Sage Publications, 1992.

Russell, Kathy, Midge Wilson, and Ronald Hall. *The Color Complex*. New York: Harcourt Brace Jovanovich, 1992.

Sándor, Gabrielle. "The Other Americans." *American Demographics* 16(6):36–43, June 1994.

Schwerner, Cassie. "Beyond Socialism and Identity Politics: The U.S. Left after the Fall." Pp. 32–45 in *What's Left*, ed. Charles Derber, Amherst, Mass.: The University of Massachusetts Press, 1995.

Sege, Irene. "Color Her World." *Boston Globe*, January, 18, 1995, p. A1.

Shalim, Dmitri. "Modernity, Postmodernism, and Pragmatist Inquiry: An Introduction." *Symbolic Interaction* 16(4):303–32, 1993.

Sickels, Robert J. *Race, Marriage and the Law*. Albuquerque: University of New Mexico Press, 1972.

Simmel, Georg. *The Sociology of Georg Simmel*, trans. Kurt H. Wolff. Glencoe, Ill.: The Free Press, 1950.

———. *The Web of Group Affiliations*, trans. by Reinhard Bendix. Glencoe, Ill.: Free Press, 1955.

Sitkoff, Harvard. *The Struggle for Black Equality 1954–1980*. New York: Hill and Wang, 1981.

Smith, Starita. "Racially 'Mixed' Seek Category in Census." *The Times Picayune*, June 2, 1996, p. A24, col.1–6.

Sowell, Thomas. "A Black Conservative Dissents," *New York Times Magazine*, August 8, 1976, p. 15.

Spickard, Paul, R. *Mixed Blood*. Madison: University of Wisconsin Press, 1989.

————. "The Illogic of American Racial Categories." Pp. 12–23 in *Racially Mixed People in America*, ed. Maria P. P. Root. Newbury Park, Calif.: Sage Publications, 1992.

Steinberg, Stephen. *The Ethnic Myth*. Boston: Beacon Press, 1989.

————. *Turning Back*. Boston: Beacon Press, 1995.

Stonequist, Everett V. *The Marginal Man*. New York: Russell & Russell, 1937/1961.

Strauss, Anselm. *Mirrors and Masks: The Search for Identity*. Glencoe, Ill.: Free Press, 1959.

Stryker, Sheldon. "Identity Salience and Role Performance." *Journal of Marriage and the Family*. 30:558–64, 1968.

————. *Symbolic Interactionism: A Social Structural Version*. Menlo Park, Calif.: Benjamin/Cummings, 1980.

————. "Commitment, Identity, Salience, and Role Behavior: Theory and Research Example." in *Personality, Roles, and Social Behavior*, ed. Ickes, William John, and Eric S. Knowles. New York: Springer-Verlag, 1982.

————. "Identity Theory: Developments and Extension." Pp. 89–104 in *Self and Society: Psychosocial Perspectives*, ed. Krysia Yardley and Terry Hones. New York: Wiley, 1987.

————. "Identity Theory." In *Encyclopedia of Sociology*, ed. Edgar F. Borgatta. New York: Macmillan, 2:871–76, 1992.

Taylor, Jerome, and John Rogers. "Relationship between Cultural Identity and Exchange Disposition." *Journal of Black Psychology*. 19(3): August 1993:248.

Terkel, Studs. *Race*. New York: The New Press, 1992.

"The Numbers Game." *Time*. Special Issue, Fall 1993, p. 12.

Thompson, Nick. "Sly Legacy of Prejudice at Colleges." *Boston Globe*, October 19, 1996, p. C1.

Tizard, Barbara, and Ann Phoenix. *Black, White or Mixed Race?* London and New York: Routledge, 1993.

Tucker, William, H. *The Science and Politics of Racial Research*. Urbana and Chicago: University of Illinois Press, 1994.

U.S. Bureau of the Census, *Statistical Abstract of the United States, 1994*. Washington, D.C.: U.S. Government Printing Office, 1994, p. 546.

————. *Statistical Abstract of the United States, 1992*. Washington, DC: US Government Printing Office, 1992, p. 393.

Vela-McConnell, James A. "Who Is My Neighbor?: Social Affinity in a Modern World," Boston College, 1997.

Walker, Samuel, et al. *The Color of Justice*. Belmont, Calif.: Wadsworth, 1996.

Wallace, Michele. *Black Macho and the Myth of the Superwoman*. New York: Dial Press, 1979.

Weigert, Andrew J., J. Smith Teitge, and Dennis W. Teitge. *Society and Identity*. Cambridge: Cambridge University Press, 1986.

Weisberger, Bernard A. "A Nation of Immigrants." *American Heritage*, February/March 1994:75–91.

West, Cornel. *Race Matters*. New York: Vintage Books, 1993.

White, Joseph L., and Thomas A. Parham. *The Psychology of Blacks*. Englewood Cliffs, N.J.: Prentice Hall, 1990.

Williamson, Joel. *New People*. New York: Free Press, 1980.

Wilson, Anne. *Mixed Race Children*. London: Allen & Unwin, 1987.

Wilson, William Julius. *The Declining Significance of Race*. Chicago: University of Chicago Press, 1987.

Winchester, Brenda-Jean. "More Than Just a Pretty Face." *Interrace Magazine*, April/May
    1995, p. 36.
X, Malcolm. *The End of White Supremacy*. New York: Arcade Publishing, 1971.
Zack, Naomi. *Race and Mixed Race*. Philadelphia: Temple University Press, 1993.
————. *American Mixed Race*. Lanham, Md.: Rowman & Littlefield Publishers, 1995.

Index

About the Author

KATHLEEN ODELL KORGEN is Assistant Professor of Sociology at William Paterson University in Wayne, New Jersey.